RYA

C000301487

by Paul Glatzel

Illustrations by Pete Galvin
Edited by Simon Jinks
and Jon Mendez

2005

Foreword

The RYA Powerboat Handbook is designed to accompany RYA powerboat courses, taught at RYA training centres around the world. It also provides a wealth of valuable information to all those thinking of going to sea.

More detailed information on specific subjects can be gained by reading:

RYA Day Skipper or Yachtmaster Shorebased Notes.
These books cover the theoretical side of navigation, seamanship, meteorology and collision avoidance (Rules of the Road). They support the RYA Day Skipper and Yachtmaster courses.

RYA Radar, RYA Electronic Navigation, RYA Weather Handbook, RYA Navigation Handbook, RYA Motor Cruising Handbook.
These books give detailed information on specific subjects and are designed to be used by all boaters.

Practical courses

There is no subsitute for experience. No matter how detailed the book, practical experience on board a boat with a trained instructor is worth its weight in gold. For the best possible preparation, use this book in conjunction with RYA tuition.

RYA practical courses include:

RYA Helmsman Course
RYA Day Skipper Course
RYA Coastal Skipper Course

© 2005 RYA
First Published 2005
The Royal Yachting Association
RYA House, Ensign Way, Hamble
Southampton SO31 4YA
Tel: 0845 345 0400
Fax: 0845 345 0329
Email: info@rya.org.uk
Web: www.rya.org.uk

British Cataloguing in Publication Date:
A Catalogue record of this book is available from the British Library.
ISBN: 0901501999
Acknowledgements: The United Kingdom Hydrographic Office, Piplers of Poole, Marinautic, Cobbs Quay Marina, The Met Office,
Photographic credits: McMurdo, Piplers of Poole, Marinautic, Garmin, Icom, RNLI, Motor Boats Monthly, Scorpion RIBs, Tim Bartlett, Amberley Marine, Jon Mendez, PPL, Paul Mara and Laurence West.
Design: Creative Byte
Printed by: Brown & Son, Ringwood
Cover Design: Pete Galvin

Key to symbols

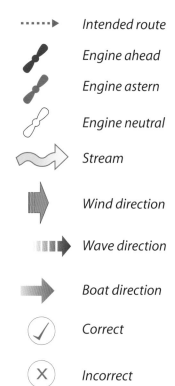

Intended route

Engine ahead

Engine astern

Engine neutral

Stream

Wind direction

Wave direction

Boat direction

Correct

Incorrect

Contents

Introduction

Powerboating is an exhilarating, fun, and often, fast activity. In recent years the number of people involved in the sport has multiplied meaning that there are many more boats on the water. It has never been more important to acquire skills to make the sport safer and more enjoyable for all.

Whether you are a beginner or an experienced powerboater, this Handbook will help develop and expand your skills. It also acts as a useful resource for the RYA National Powerboat Scheme, and covers all of the areas of the syllabus; in fact, some subjects are covered to a greater depth than the level required.

All boats work along the principles set down in this book. Whether you are fishing or cruising the coast, the same pre-start checks will have to be done before leaving port, the same safety issues will need to be considered and the same manoeuvres have to be performed to get to the open sea.

Although it would be impossible to include every imaginable scenario in this book, we hope to give you the knowledge to assess a situation correctly and make an informed decision on what to do next.

Safety, preparation and briefing are the most important points to consider when going to sea. You must be well informed and prepared before you leave harbour. If in doubt during any manoeuvre or pilotage situation, slow down and give yourself time to think the situation through. Your aim is to think, at least, one step ahead all the time, to try to anticipate what is going to happen next.

Becoming a capable and safe powerboater comes from a mixture of experience, training and common sense.

The RYA National Powerboat Scheme consists of a number of courses aimed at powerboaters with different levels of experience and different areas of interest. It is aimed at those using planing and displacement craft, both at sea and on inland waterways. The course generally suits vessels up to about 10m, at which point the RYA Motor Cruising Scheme courses become relevant.

The RYA Motor Cruising Scheme courses are aimed at those using motor cruisers. These are typically planing or displacement craft, with accommodation, 10m and upwards in length either with single or twin-engined installations. The scheme consists of Day Skipper, Coastal Skipper and Yachtmaster courses. These are available as both theory and practical courses. The theory courses are an excellent way to develop the theoretical knowledge before taking the practical courses.

Inevitably there is no clear divide between the Motor Cruising and Powerboat Schemes, and those seeking courses on craft around the *cut-off* point should chat to both a Motor Cruising school and a Powerboat school to find out which course suits their boating requirements.

Helping you get started
and get going -
whatever your age or experience

Level 1 INTRODUCTION TO POWERBOATING
A practical introduction to boat handling skills for the beginner.

Level 2 NATIONAL POWERBOAT COURSE
Be competent – learn the essentials to be a skilled Powerboat driver (Also the basis of the International Certificate of Competence; Power up to 10m).

Intermediate – POWERBOAT DAY CRUISING COURSE
Going somewhere? Pilotage and passage planning by day on coastal waters, using both traditional and electronic navigational techniques.

Advanced – POWERBOAT DAY AND NIGHT COURSE
For the adventurous cruiser - essential skills and safety considerations for skippering a boat by night, in unfamiliar waters, and boat handling in more demanding conditions.

SAFETY BOAT COURSE
Boat handling & positioning skills, towing, and safety considerations when acting as a safety boat, escort craft, or coach boat for racing or training activities.

PERSONAL WATERCRAFT CERTIFICATE
Have fun aboard a Personal Watercraft safely. A one day course covering how to handle a PW at low and high speed and the essentials of safety afloat.

RYA / MCA Advanced Powerboat Certificate of Competence
This is gained by examination which is conducted by RYA Advanced Powerboat Examiners. Examinations are open to anyone with the required experience.

RYA courses are safe, informative and enjoyable. They are run at inspected sites by qualified instructors; look for the tick mark logo.

For more information visit www.rya.org.uk

1 | Parts of a Boat

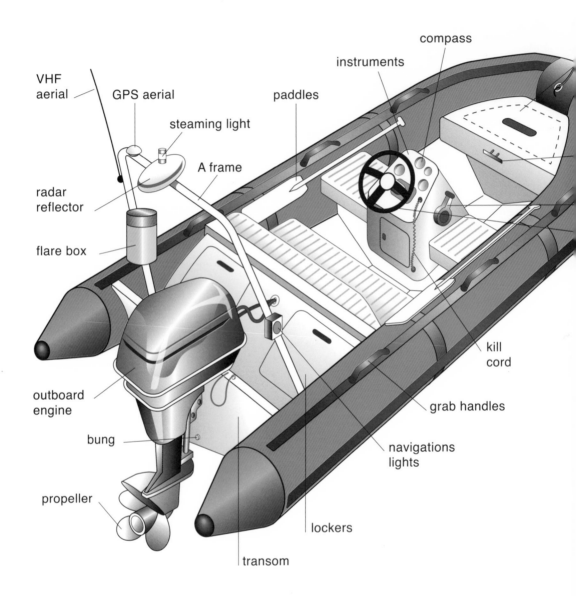

VHF aerial

GPS aerial

steaming light

A frame

radar reflector

flare box

outboard engine

bung

propeller

paddles

instruments

compass

kill cord

grab handles

navigations lights

lockers

transom

RIB (Rigid Inflatable Boat)

outdrive

propeller

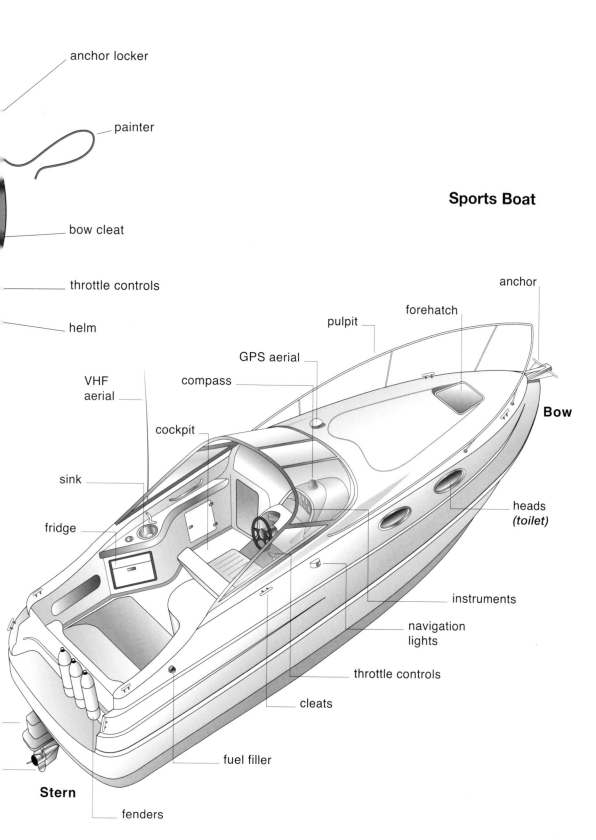

anchor locker

painter

Sports Boat

bow cleat

throttle controls

anchor

forehatch

helm

pulpit

GPS aerial

VHF
aerial

compass

Bow

cockpit

sink

heads
(toilet)

fridge

instruments

navigation
lights

throttle controls

cleats

fuel filler

Stern

fenders

2 | Types of Boats, Engines and Hulls

It is possible to have as much fun in a four metre boat as in a large twin-engine fast cruiser. Your choice of boat depends on its intended use and where it is to be used. Problems will arise if a boat is not used for its designed purpose, or used in areas where sea conditions are far worse than those intended for its design. When choosing a boat you should consider where you intend to use it, and what for.

Choosing a boat

There are a number of factors to consider when choosing a boat:

- Intended use: A boat used for fishing in the winter is somewhat different to a boat used for water-skiing in the summer. Each boat is designed with a particular use in mind and it is important to choose one that will meet your needs.

- Boat budget: Boating is perceived as being expensive, but it need not be. A small second-hand powerboat can be bought for the same price as a PC system and can be an ideal starter boat. A large budget need not mean more enjoyment.

- Running costs: Buying the boat is only the first part of the cost. Fuel, equipment and storage should also be budgeted for. Fuel will usually cost more afloat and there can be a large difference in costs between diesel and petrol. To store the boat in a marina, boat park or have the trailer serviced can cost a small fortune. While insurance and servicing plus the initial outlay on safety equipment can all bite a large chunk out of your bank balance. Do your sums and get quotes on running costs before buying.

- Area of use: The intended area of operation will be a major consideration. An area with a strong tidal race and often choppy conditions requires a boat with the hull characteristics, strength and power to deal with them. The same boat used on an inland lake may well be slow when compared with other boats on the lake. Equally, boating in an area where quayside petrol is unavailable may influence your decision to buy a diesel engined boat.

In some countries boats are categorised by the type of water they are to be used on;

Sheltered waters Boats that operate in daylight only, in estuaries, inshore or inland waters, close to a safe harbour of refuge where shelter may be found within approximately one hour if the weather should worsen. Boats in this category are likely to be around 6m or less in length.

Inshore Boats that cruise along the coast, within ten miles of land and approximately four hours of passage time from a safe harbour or refuge in which shelter may be found, by day or night.

Offshore Boats that cruise around the coast and to different countries, making offshore passages of between 50 and 500 miles. Boats in this category are likely to be over 8m.

Boats with hull shape

Dory hulls offer a reduced wetted area than 'V' hulls and plane easily. However, they tend to 'slam' into waves and are only suitable for inshore use. They are mainly found on sheltered waters and are very stable. The hull has a deeper 'V' forward, that flattens out aft. This gives better action through waves and good planing features.

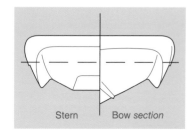

Stern | Bow *section*

Dory Stable flat bottomed boat with good speed in flat water. Good load bearing design but little grip in the water during turns. Excellent for lakes and sheltered waters.

Displacement hulls tend to be far more rounded and work by pushing water out of the way as they move. They tend to be slow, but very seaworthy. Their speed is governed by waterline length.

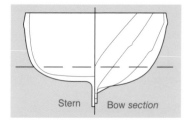

Stern | Bow *section*

Displacement boats are generally safe and slow boats with inboard engines. They may offer accommodation and some luxuries. Their speed is governed by the length of boat in the water but offer good sea-keeping qualities.

Catamarans have two hulls giving excellent stability and load carrying capabilities, requiring less power for the equivalent size vessel for similar performance.

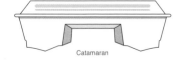

Catamaran

Catamarans are used as small ferries and fishing boats. They are also found on race boats as the reduced wetted surface area allows greater speed.

'V' shaped hulls are good in waves and rougher conditions. A deep 'V' hull slices through waves but tends to have less internal space because they have less beam (width). A flatter 'V' has a better beam but compromises its ability to slice through waves and may slam.

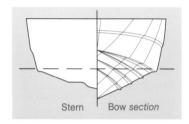

Stern | Bow *section*

Speedboat (4–8m) Small, fast, good for water-skiing and a family runabout. Hulls vary from very deep 'V' (generally boats with an offshore pedigree) to a flatter 'V', which potentially have better interior space due to a wider beam. Smaller boats mainly have outboards and most over 6m have inboard engines with an outdrive.

Fast fishers A popular style of boat due to its suitability for choppier coastal waters. They offer a sheltered wheelhouse, large open decked area at the rear. Although designed for coastal fishing they are also suitable as a family day boat. Some have fairly deep 'V' hulls that have the ability to cope with rougher conditions. Available with both outboard and inboard engines.

RIB- Rigid Inflatable Boat Designed initially for rescue and safety work, but increasingly popular as a family boat. Hull types range from deep 'V' to far flatter hulls. In competent hands, a well designed RIB can handle seas far in excess of those handled by other comparable sized boats due to their design and buoyant tubes. Lengths vary from 3m to 10m. Over 7m and inboard engines become available – almost exclusively diesel.

Fast Cruiser A great family boat offering a good mix of accommodation and deck area. Always inboard and mostly diesel fuelled. Upwards of 8m twin engine installations are quite common. The high topsides increase their windage, so care needs to be taken when berthing.

Engines and drives

Outboards Outboard engines are by far the most common engine and drive system on small powerboats. The major advantage is that they are a self contained engine, drive and steering system that can be easily removed for service or replaced without much skilled work. Outboards are nearly exclusively petrol/gasoline powered.

Outdrives In effect, the lower part of the outboard is bolted onto the transom of the boat, but the engine is inside the boat. This is the most popular option for medium to large size powerboats as it allows for better weight distribution by placing the engine inboard. Also the engine gets better protection from the elements and is easier to service in the boat. The outdrive leg is steered left or right using a wheel.

Shaft drives Shaft drives are common on ski and working boats and increasingly on some of the small fast fishing type craft. A shaft drive allows the engine to be positioned further forward to aid the interior design or weight distribution. The propeller shaft attaches to the engine, runs through waterproof through-hull fittings to the propeller. A separate rudder is used to steer the boat using thrust from the propeller.

Jet drives The positioning of engine and drive unit is similar to that of an outdrive. But this time the engine drives an impellor (paddlewheel), that sucks in water through a grille and jets it out under high pressure through a small hole to produce thrust. A steerable nozzle directs the jet of water to give power and steerage.

Twin-engined installations

Boats, such as large RIBs and racing boats have twin outboards. Twin outdrive or shaft installations are usually the preserve of boats over 8m. Depending on the particular circumstances this offers more power and a safety net should one engine fail. A key feature of twin-engined installations is the ability of a craft to turn within its own length at slow speed by running each engine opposite directions – one ahead and one astern. This turning effect is limited where the separation of the engines is much less than 1m.

Pros and cons of types of outboard

The choice of outboard engine is between 2-stroke and 4-stroke petrol/gasoline engines.

Here are some comparisons:

4-Stroke	2-Stroke
• Very good fuel economy and very quiet running. • Oil is permanently in the engine crankcase like a car engine. • Sizes are available from a 2hp to 300hp.	• Lighter than comparable 4–strokes, so a better power to weight ratio. • Most 2-strokes are less fuel efficient than 4-strokes, newer models are getting better. • Oil is consumed and is either added to the fuel or kept in an oil reservoir.

Outboard engines

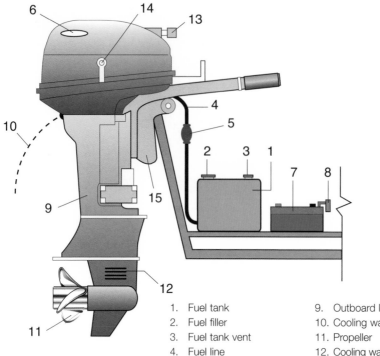

1. Fuel tank
2. Fuel filler
3. Fuel tank vent
4. Fuel line
5. Fuel bulb
6. Oil filler
7. Starter battery
8. Battery isolator switch
9. Outboard leg
10. Cooling water tell-tale
11. Propeller
12. Cooling water inlet grille
13. Engine hand-start
14. Gear-operating lever
15. Transom mounting
    bracket

Throttle system

1. Single lever control
2. Fast idle control (some boats only)
3. Kill cord
4. Ignition switch
5. Gear lever interlock

Tip - always attach the Kill Cord to yourself when the engine is running.

Inboard engines

These tend to be available on craft 6m upwards and are usually found on sportsboats over 7m and all sports cruisers. Single engines are used up to 8m; above this twin installations are more popular. Either outdrives or shafts depending on the boat.

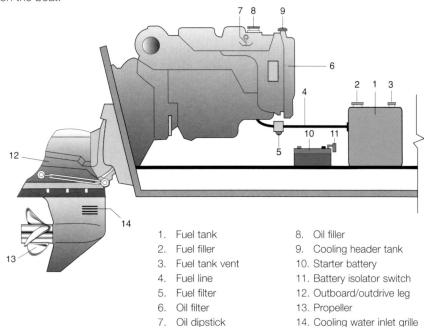

1. Fuel tank
2. Fuel filler
3. Fuel tank vent
4. Fuel line
5. Fuel filter
6. Oil filter
7. Oil dipstick
8. Oil filler
9. Cooling header tank
10. Starter battery
11. Battery isolator switch
12. Outboard/outdrive leg
13. Propeller
14. Cooling water inlet grille

Inboards vs. outboards

In most cases, the decision is determined by the boat you buy, although larger RIBs and some of the fast fishers often give you the option.

Inboards	Outboards
• Available in petrol or diesel.	• Far more reliable than in the past.
• Diesel may be the preferable option when waterside petrol is not easily available.	• Too complex for anything other than basic troubleshooting.
• Can be cheaper and simpler to service as they are essentially marinised car or truck engines.	• Can be raised out of the water at rest to prevent weed growth.
• Often provide a sundeck area above the engine.	• Far better power to weight ratio than comparable inboards.
	• Diesel outboards are available, although rare.
	• Possible to remove outboards for easier servicing.

Throttle systems

There is a variety of throttle controls available. Most operate using control cables to the engine. Electronic controls using electrical signals down a wire are becoming more common. Most outboard engines have a small safety catch which needs to be engaged to allow the throttle to be used. Throttle systems are very basic. They allow forward drive, reverse drive or neutral to be engaged. Pushing the throttle 'forward' increases power to quicken the boat's speed through the water.

Starting procedure

The engine starting procedure varies from boat to boat, so this section acts only as a guide. Depending on how, and where, you launch and start your boat, many of these checks can be carried out beforehand.

Consult the owner's manual for starting instructions specific to your boat. Engines and throttle systems vary but the pre-start checks may include:

Pre-start checks	*Starting*
• Check fuel level and fuel turned on.	• On outboards - squeeze bulb to prime fuel.
• Turn batteries on.	• Attach kill cord to yourself.
• Check engine oil level.	• Ensure that engine is in neutral.
• Check drive leg and trim-tab oil levels.	• Engage choke.
• Check coolant level.	• Set throttle control to 'Fast Idle'.
• Check drive belts for condition and tension.	• Check prop is clear.
• Check raw water filter is clear of weed and obstructions.	• Start engine.
• Ensure air vent on tank is open.	• Check cooling water 'tell tale'.
• Vent engine bay using blower.	• Reduce throttle as engine warms.
	• Engage gears briefly to check operation.

Bowthrusters

Bowthrusters are increasingly common on boats under 10m. The bowthruster is controlled from a joystick on the helm and pushes the bow of the boat either to port or starboard. They are used to neatly bring the bow alongside a pontoon or improve the angle of approach at slow speed. Only a small amount of power is needed, otherwise too much movement is created. Think of them as an aid to perfection rather than a solution to bad boat-handling.

Fuel Choice

When choosing a boat with an inboard engine there may be a choice between petrol or diesel engines. Here are some comparisons between petrol and diesel engines.

Petrol	Diesel
• Petrol engines are less expensive to buy.	• Diesel inboards are more expensive than petrol engines to buy.
• The fire risk is higher.	• Fire risk is lower.
• Operating costs are often higher due to the greater cost of fuel and poorer economy, many direct injection engines are more economic.	• High usage will often make the extra initial investment of a diesel engine worthwhile.
• Sometimes refuelling via cans is the only and often impractical option.	• Diesel engines are generally more reliable and safer than petrol engines.
• Trailered boats can fill up at petrol stations instead of afloat.	• They are usually heavier than petrol and their power to weight ratio is less.
• Petrol engines require a qualified mechanic on all but the simplest problems.	• Many diesel engines operate using simple engineering that can be fixed at sea.
• They require electrics to run and the damp atmosphere onboard can hinder operation.	

3 | Propellers

The propeller transmits the power from the engine to create propulsion.

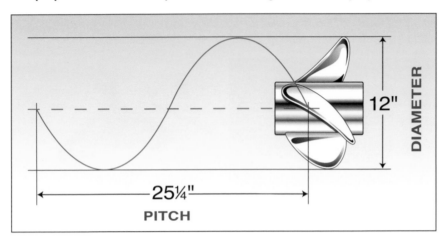

Pitch and diameter

Props are measured by their pitch and diameter.
- Diameter is the actual diameter of the propeller and blades and usually increases with engine size.

- Pitch is the theoretical distance the craft will travel on one rotation of the propeller. The actual distance travelled will be less due to slippage.

- Both pitch and diameter are generally measured in inches, however some metric dimensions are now being used.

Types of propeller

- Aluminium is the most common material for outdrive and outboard propellers. It is cost effective but can be easily damaged if it comes into contact with hard objects. However, the blades can usually be repaired fairly cheaply by a specialist.

- Stainless steel propellers are far stronger, can withstand more abuse, but are more expensive. The extra strength allows the blades to be thinner than their aluminium equivalents, which improves performance. However, should the propeller strike a hard object, the force can be transmitted through into the gearbox and may cause damage.

- Composite props are increasingly common, especially as spares. Some even allow blades to be replaced if one becomes chipped.

- Bronze props are commonly found on shaft drive craft such as ski-boats.

- Surface piercing props are the domain of race boats and high performance craft, and are designed for top-end speed. Optimum performance is acheived when only the lower half of the propeller is in the water.

How many blades?

- Three blades - Offer good top speed but less low down punch for acceleration.

- Four blades - Offer very good low-end acceleration, good for pulling skiers or working in rough conditions, but at the slight expense of top-end speed.

- Duoprops have two contra-rotating props on one shaft and usually two three-bladed propellers. This allows greater performance and the elimination of prop-walk. In effect the pitch is twice that of a normally propped boat, therefore it tries to drive forward twice as much for the same revs, doubling the efficiency.

Choosing a propeller

Finding the best propeller for your boat depends on your boating needs. Most people will be more than happy with the prop that is fitted to the boat as standard. Sometimes, because of how you use the boat, it may be worth changing the prop to increase efficiency. If you are constantly pulling skiers, choose a prop that gives you more torque at low power. If you were solely focussed on speed, you should choose a prop that may be slow to get onto the plane but achieves a higher top speed. For some boaters, choosing and changing a propeller to optimise performance becomes a pastime in itself, but for most, the prop originally fitted by the engine manufacturer is satisfactory.

Propeller problems

Ventilation When exhaust gases or air from the surface are drawn onto the blades of a rotating propeller it may fail to grip and may rotate rapidly with a sudden increase in revs and loss of speed. This can give rise to cavitation.

Cavitation Occurs when the pressure at the blades of the propeller drops, allowing water on the blades to boil creating minute air bubbles. These bubbles contain considerable energy and, as they break down, can literally eat away at the blades' surface. Stainless props, being far stronger, can withstand this attack better, and are less susceptible as the blades are thinner.

4 | Safety and Planning

'Safety is a matter of common sense and state of mind', however once you decide to go afloat, there are a number of things to consider; the type of boat, how to handle it and how to plan and execute trips safely. As the skipper of a powerboat you are responsible for the safety of your crew, and boat. Having a great time on the water starts with good preparation and planning. This includes preparing the boat, ensuring the weather is suitable, briefing your crew and checking that you have the correct equipment for your intended passage.

We all have a responsibility to other water users to ensure we operate the boat sensibly and in harmony with others. Keep wash to a minimum around other craft, stay well clear of moored craft, sailboats and canoes and stay to the correct side in narrow channels.

Planning your day

Weather

Weather is discussed in more depth in chapter 19. However, the key issue is should you go to sea in the first place? Use various sources of information to understand the conditions you will face. Take into account the experience of yourself, your crew and the capabilities of your boat. If you are in any doubt, do not go. Making this decision is not always easy, but as skipper you are responsible for everyone's safety.

Where to go

This is governed by many factors, but make sure you choose an area suitable for your boating needs and level of experience. If you are trailing a boat, check if a launch site a few miles further on may provide easier and safer launching and more sheltered sea conditions. Contact local marinas, chandlers and tourist centres for advice.

Many harbours and ports have their own local bylaws covering:

- Speed limits and quiet areas.
- Approved water-ski and jet-ski areas.
- Local collision regulations.

These can be obtained from harbour offices and marinas.

Personal equipment:

If in sunny climates ensure you take adequate protection from the sun, include long sleeved shirts and hats. Wet and cold climates are made worse by wind chill exacerbated by the speed of the boat. Consider taking; helmets, gloves, dry suits and waterproof clothing. Children get cold very quickly, so plan your trips accordingly.

- Sun cream (high protection factor); medication (and instructions); water; snacks; waterproofs, warm clothing; personal buoyancy; suitable footwear; sunglasses; sun hat; towel.

Boat equipment

You do not need to spend a fortune equipping a boat. It is more important to have the correct safety gear than the latest electronic gizmo. Inexpensive purchases can be made via: boat jumbles, web based auction sites, mail order catalogues or simply by shopping around the multitude of chandler's shops. The equipment carried depends on the intended area of use. It is vitally important the both you and the crew know how to operate the safety equipment. Ensure the equipment is stored in dry and accessible places and consider marking lockers containing important items so that everything can be found easily.

Some items will depend on the area and particular use of the boat. Items to consider including the following.

Boat equipment: anchor with warp (rope) and chain, radar reflector, kill cord and a spare, tool kit and engine spares, compass, mobile phone, flares, fire extinguisher(s), a fire blanket, lifejackets or buoyancy aids, bilge pump or bailer, charts, watch or clock, first-aid kit, GPS (not essential but useful), hull repair kit (e.g. wooden bungs) or tube repair kit, paddles or auxiliary outboard, mooring warps and fenders, throwing line, water, navigation-lights, horn, relevant shapes. VHF radio (fixed or hand-held), knife, almanac.

Extra equipment for longer offshore trips: Danbuoy marker (for man overboard), Navtex radio receiver, EPIRB, hand-held VHF, barometer, depth sounder, GPS/chart plotter, hand-bearing compass, binoculars, liferaft.

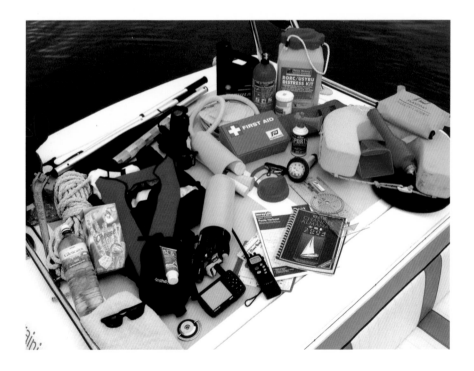

Kill cord

Most powerboats have an engine cut-out device called a kill cord. One end is attached near the throttle and other around the helmsman's leg. If the helmsman falls out of the boat, the engine cuts out. Runaway powerboats have caused serious injury and death. Test your kill cord to ensure it works. Spare kill cords should be carried so the boat can be re-started and driven back to the person in the water. Attach the cord around your leg or buoyancy aid and not to your wrist.

Lifejackets and buoyancy aids

A lifejacket is designed to turn an unconscious casualty in the water face up, keeping their head up out of the water. A buoyancy aid will keep a person afloat but will not turn them face up.

Lifejackets

Most adult lifejackets are gas inflation models, and are comfortable to wear and easy to store. Inflation is by a small gas canister and is activated manually or automatically when in contact with the water. Lifejackets are good all round performers and excellent for children and anyone less confident in water.

Auto and manual gas inflation: A person entering the water unconscious is unable to inflate a manual gas inflation lifejacket, therefore auto lifejackets are generally preferable. However some auto lifejackets can inflate accidentally if they become wet.

Make sure your lifejacket has crotch-straps. This keeps the lifejacket in the correct position and prevents you falling out of it in the water. At night, ensure lifejacket lights are fitted.

Regularly check your lifejacket, they should also be serviced annually. The manufacturer will supply you with detailed maintenance procedures. Part of your check should include:

- Abrasion damage to the inflatable chamber.
- Gas inflation cylinder, for signs of corrosion.
- Gas inflation cylinder, for tightness of connection to inflation mechanism.
- The trigger mechanism, for damage.

Buoyancy aids

These provide buoyancy but will not turn an unconscious casualty upright, or provide as much support as a lifejacket. They are designed for watersports such as dinghy sailing, windsurfing and waterskiing. Often worn by powerboat drivers on safety boat duty overseeing a race or training, they are useful in smaller boats where having both lifejackets and buoyancy aids are impractical.

Skipper's responsibilities

As a skipper you have responsibility for your crew, their safety and well being. Before departure, ensure you are made aware of any medical conditions your crew may have, where their medication is kept and how it is administered.

You should have a basic knowledge of first aid, best acquired through a recognised first aid course.

Safety briefing

Once ready to go afloat, give your crew a safety briefing covering the following:

- Use of lifejackets.

- Use of flares.

- Use of VHF - how to send a Mayday message.

- First aid list locations.

- Engine starting procedure and kill-cord use.

- Basic boat handling - so that they can get back to you if you go overboard.

- Anchoring.

Deck brief

Before departure go through the basics of tying up. Take the time to practise tying up and coming alongside. Explain well in advance what you are doing.

Keeping your crew informed and involved will help them enjoy the experience, but will only be acheived if they know what they are supposed to do.

Once out at sea, do remember that even though you may love going fast, your crew may not be so confident, and they could become frightened. You know what you are going to do – your crew don't, so throttle back and introduce them slowly to your sport.

Summoning assistance

If a problem arises, you should know what action to take and how to deal with it. Your first consideration is: are you, the crew or boat in immediate danger? If yes, call for assistance immediately.

The most common methods for raising the alarm where there is grave and imminent danger are:

• A VHF radio Mayday call.

• Flares.

• Arm signals, sound horn, mobile phone.

If the problem is less serious, as an example your engine has stopped working, you may well flag down another boat, call the Coastguard or a boatyard on either VHF or a mobile phone to arrange for a tow.

VHF radio

How you raise the alarm using VHF depends on whether the radio is equipped with Digital Selective Calling (DSC). This allows some messages including a Mayday to be initially automatically broadcast digitally, rather than by voice. A DSC radio should receive position information from a GPS (Global Positioning System). At the touch of a button, the nature of the alert, the craft's identity and position is sent out in a fraction of a second.

DSC radio

• Remove the cover on the red 'Distress' button and press the red button for 5 seconds.

• A digital alert is broadcast to all DSC-equipped craft and the local Coastguard Station.

• The alert can include your MMSI - a unique number identifying your craft, your position and the time.

• On Channel 16 broadcast the voice Mayday call and message (overleaf):

Mayday, Mayday, Mayday.
This is powerboat Fleetwood, Fleetwood, Fleetwood,
Mayday Fleetwood,
MMSI 234001234.
My position is 50° 30'.5N, 001° 57'.5W, approximately 5 miles south of Anvil Point, Have hit submerged object and am sinking.
Four persons on board.
Abandoning to the liferaft.
Over.

- Release the transmit button.

- You will immediately receive a digital reply from the Coastguard, followed by a voice reply on Channel 16.

- No other stations should use Channel 16 while the Coastguard is 'casualty working'.

Non-DSC radio

Follow the voice procedure outlined above for the Mayday call on Channel 16 but without the MMSI number.

If your predicament is less serious than a Mayday situation, the coastguard will still assist you if you call with "DSC Urgency Alert", followed by a Pan Pan call on Channel 16. A 'Pan Pan' call indicates that you require assistance but that there is no immediate danger to life. It is also used if a person on board requires medical attention or advice.

It is an offence to use a VHF Radio without a license. Contact your National Boating Authority for details of VHF courses.

Mobile phone

A mobile phone can in some situations be useful. In an emergency, calling the emergency services and asking for the Coastguard will connect you to the local Coastguard Operations Room. Programme the phone numbers of local organisations and friends who could offer assistance. Remember, mobile phones are not usually waterproof and reception depends on cell coverage which can be patchy at sea. A SMS text message will have a better chance of getting through.

> **Tip** - When stating your position, quote the position as a 'lat and long' taken from your chart or GPS, e.g., 50° 30'.5N, 001° 57'.5W, also explain it in simple terms as "approximately 5 miles south of Anvil Point". More craft will then know where you are and be able to offer assistance.

Flares

Flares are an essential item of safety equipment but there are many different types and makes and a variety of ways they operate. Familiarise yourself with their operation. It is good practice to carry only one make of flare on board to prevent confusion when you need to use them.

Recommended number to carry		Inshore	Sheltered waters
	Red parachute flare The most effective long range flare; projects a bright flare to about 300m. Do not use near helicopters!	2	0
	Red hand-held flare Indicates precise position of craft, use when close to other craft or land.	4	2
	Orange hand-held smoke Use in daylight, useful for attracting helicopter or lifeboat attention.	2	2
	White hand-held Collision-avoidance flare; use to alert other craft to your presence.	4	0

Tip - Flares have an expiry date 3-4 years from manufacture. Ensure your flares are in date.

Stow flares in a waterproof box. Place foam at the bottom and around the sides to soften impact on the flares. A pair of gardening gloves will help protect hands when handling them.

Attend a flare demonstration or course where you can let off real flares.

Launch and Recovery

Unless the boat is kept in a marina berth, launching and recovery by trailer will be a key aspect of where to go afloat. The decision on which slipway to use depends on the type of boat, the needs and interests of your crew and security for the vehicle and trailer while you are afloat.

Launching

Go to any public slipway and you will see plenty of examples of safe and easy launches alongside some dangerous and stressful ones: the difference being good planning and preparation.

Planning

- Where will you launch? Some slipways are public and free, many are privately owned and a fee must be paid.

- Check if there are local bylaws to consider, some areas allow only certain types or sizes of boats.

- In some areas a permit is required to use a boat.

- Some slipways are suitable only for smaller craft, while others have a walkway or dock alongside, making launching easier. Others end abruptly leaving the trailer wheels stuck in the mud at low water.

- Ensure your tow vehicle will cope. Rear wheel drive vehicles will struggle on a slippery slope, while front wheel drives suffer from wheel spin if the weight of the trailer is excessive. Choose the slipway and launch method which suits your vehicle.

- Check the local tide tables in advance to ensure you have enough water for launching and recovery.

- Are conditions safe for launching? Strong winds, especially if they are blowing onshore, can make a launch very difficult and dangerous.

Preparation

- On arrival, park well away from the slip.

- Remove the tailboard straps and boat cover.

- Insert the bung and check the hull for damage in transit.

- Load the boat with equipment and supplies.

After a long journey let the wheel bearings cool for 45 minutes before launching. Immersing wheel bearings earlier may create a vacuum as the bearings rapidly cool, this draws in water and washes out the grease from the bearings.

Launching

How far the trailer is reversed into the water depends on the gradient of the slipway, the size and weight of boat, and how easy it is to launch from the trailer. The rear of the boat needs to float so that it can be reversed or pushed off the trailer. Car wheels are best kept well away from sea water.

- Manoeuvre the trailer to the top of the slipway.

- Reverse down the slipway if possible only partially submerging the trailer's wheels (to preserve the bearings and brakes) then push the boat off the trailer or hop into the boat and reverse it away.

If the gradient of the slipway is shallow which prevents you launching with the trailer attached to the car, use a rope or metal extension bar to enable the trailer to be reversed further into the water.

- At the top of the slipway, disconnect the trailer, lower the jockey wheel and put the handbrake on.

- Connect a long line between the trailer and the tow hook using bowlines.

- Drive the car forwards to take up the slack in the line. Remove the handbrake and slowly reverse down the slipway while an assistant keeps the trailer in line.

- The assistant may need to enter the water to ease the boat off.

Tip - Launching with a rope between the vehicle and trailer can be useful to keep the tow vehicle's wheels clear of the lower slippery part of the slipway and water.

Danger - To avoid the boat sliding off the trailer when backing down the slipway; ensure the winch strap remains attached to the boat.

Recovery

In many instances it is possible to stop the boat whilst drifting towards the slip, jump out when the water is shallow enough and hold the boat until the trailer comes into the water. On other occasions, especially where the slip is steep, it is best to drive the boat onto the trailer.

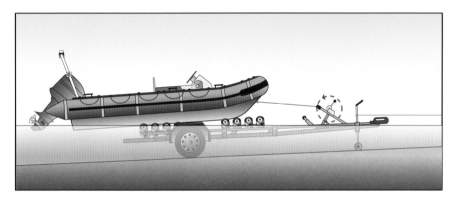

Driving onto a trailer

This technique requires careful throttle control and more care is required than with a manual recovery. The helmsman, needs to line up the approach to the trailer compensating for wind and stream, arriving at the trailer so that the forward 'V' of the hull aligns centrally on the trailer.

- Ease the trailer into the water so that it is partially submerged and allows the boat to drive on to it.

- Trim the engine up so that the prop does not ground on approach, ensure that cooling water is still circulating.

- Drive the boat on to the trailer compensating for wind and stream.

- For safety reasons you should get out of the boat when it is towed out of the water.

- When the boat is on the trailer, either attach the winch strap to the forward D ring or lash a line from the boat to the trailer.

- If a rope or bar was used, chock the wheels and reattach the vehicle to the trailer.

- Ideally, flush the engine cooling system (see page 34) with fresh water and give the boat and trailer a hose down.

If your engine does not have a dedicated flushing point, use a hose attached to muffs to direct fresh water to the intake. Start the engine and run in neutral for three to four minutes. Check your engine manual for 'care after use' details.

Danger - If launching or recovering with the trailer detached from the tow vehicle, ensure the trailer is well in the water before pushing the boat off or winching it on. The nose of the trailer can be forced rapidly skywards as the weight transfers to the rear of the trailer.

Serious injury can occur when boats roll off trailers with the winch strap attached and the winch handle rotating rapidly. Use the safety lock to prevent this happening. Never grab a winch handle if it is spinning.

Before towing

- Ensure the boat is fully secure on the trailer.

- Use tie-down straps on the D-rings on the transom to hold the rear of the boat to the trailer.

- Connect the D-ring on the bow to hold the front of the boat in position.

- Use a safety chain between the vehicle and the trailer as the two may become detached.

Tip - Steep slipways and heavy boats can cause serious harm; so take things slowly. Plan what you are going to do and double check everything before you start. Remember a good launch is one that is slow, controlled and safe.

Boat Handling | 6

Being able to helm a powerboat safely and with confidence starts with an understanding of the way a boat handles and how the elements of wind and stream affect its behaviour. Experience and practice will build your level of confidence. This section will show you how to get the most from your boat in a variety of situations.

The basics

A powerboat is moved forwards or backwards by the rotation of the propeller which pushes or pulls the boat through the water. Increase the throttle and the boat will move more as the prop turns faster. Engaging forward gear creates forward effort by thrust coming from the prop or drive-unit. Engaging neutral stops the thrust, however you may still be moving forwards due to momentum. Engaging reverse (astern) rotates the propeller in the opposite direction to stop the boat or move it astern. The steering wheel diverts the water flow from the propeller to turn the boat by turning the outboard, outdrive or rudder. Several other factors need to be considered before you start.

Pivot points

In forward gear, boats pivot at a position approximately just forward of the centre of the boat. In reverse the pivot point is near the stern of the boat, the engine in effect 'pulls' the craft around. You are turning the back of the boat and it takes a while for the front to react. These differences in handling can be used to good effect by a skipper when handling at slow speed around a marina or near pontoons.

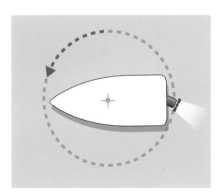 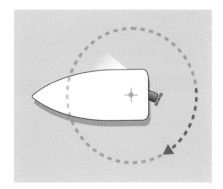

Propwalk

Propellers push the boat forward, but because of their rotation they also make the stern move to one side. This effect is called prop walk, because of the tendency of the prop to "walk" the stern to one side. It is most evident when going astern. All boats have prop-walk, and prop and hull design dictate its effect on the handling characteristics of the boat. However, propwalk on outboards is negligible.

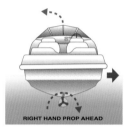

RIGHT HAND PROP AHEAD

Going astern, a right-handed prop will walk to the left (port). Some boats will walk around in a large circle whilst going astern, while others have negligible prop walk and reverse in a straight line. In use, the forward prop effect will be hardly noticed – the overriding effect on the boat will be the 'kick-to-port' in astern, and most close-quarter manoeuvres will be affected by this, especially on single prop vessels.

RIGHT HAND PROP ASTERN

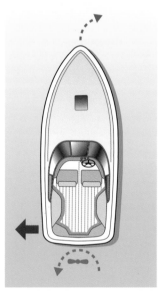

Tip - Check for prop walk whilst tied alongside. Ensure the rudder is straight, engage astern gear and observe which side the wash comes out from under the hull. Wash to starboard suggests a kick to port in astern. It is useful to establish which way a single prop boat kicks before manoeuvring out of the berth.

Streams

Streams are caused by either tide, natural river flow or by local movement of water, as occurs around locks. Streams have a similar effect to stepping onto a conveyor belt, moving you bodily in one direction.

If you motor in the same direction as the stream, the boat travels quicker past the shore and reaches its destination faster. If motoring against the stream it will take longer to reach your destination. Even though you may be travelling through the water at the same speed, your speed over ground will be less.

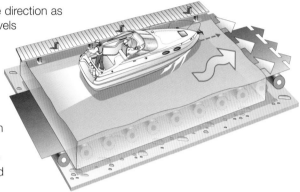

When coming alongside a boat pointing into the stream is slower over the ground retaining good steerageway, allowing better control.

Stream can also push you into or away from danger. To assess the stream's direction, look for its signs:

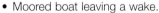

- Bubbles in the water flowing past a moored boat.

- Moored boat leaving a wake.

- Tight mooring lines indicating pressure from one side.

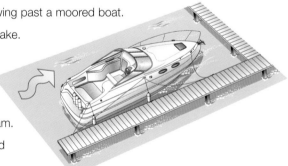

- Weed on the pontoon floats flowing down-stream.

- Water stacking up around piles and buoys.

If you are still unsure of stream direction, motor slowly across the water and look ahead at two points in line to check for drift. It is worth noting that the stream can be stronger further from the shore, and that there is sometimes a reduction in its rate in a marina or dock. When both wind and stream are opposing each other, assess which is the stronger by motoring slowly across the stream and gauging which way the boat is being pushed.

Wind

The forces of wind and stream have an effect on how the boat manoeuvres. Because planing boats have very little grip on the water, the wind can easily blow them across the water's surface. Displacement boats may be affected less by wind but more by stream.

Be aware of wind direction. You can assess the wind direction by looking at:

- Flags around the dock.

- Wind indicators at the top of yacht masts.

- Wind ruffling the surface of the water.

- By fitting a flag or wind indicator to your boat.

The effect wind has on a boat is twofold.

• Firstly, if the boat is moving slowly or has stopped, wind drifts the whole boat sideways. Sideways drift can be used to advantage in some coming alongside techniques. Good spacial awareness is required to avoid drifting downwind and onto obstructions.

• Secondly, because the bow has less grip in the water than the stern (where the props and rudders are), the wind will always blow the bow away first. Therefore it is quite difficult to keep a motor cruiser bow into the wind. Left to lie naturally, it will sit beam to wind or with the wind on one quarter.

• The easiest way to hold position in wind is to reverse gently and sit stern to wind. Reversing moves the pivot point aft. The stern will seek the wind and the bow can be allowed to blow downwind.

Tip - Use stream and wind to advantage to aid manoeuvring. Find out which has the greatest effect and use it as a brake.

Turning principals

Single shaft A single shaft drive boat is turned using bursts of ahead and astern. These bursts are applied only when the wheel is turned hard over.

Outboards Steer the boat when the propeller is moving. If the boat is moving through the water without power, the outboard has little effect as a rudder.

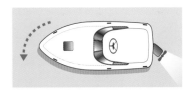

Outdrives These have similar characteristics to an outboard but the engine is inside the craft.

Twin outdrives The outside engine has greater leverage. This can be used to good effect in a turn. To turn hard to port, turn the wheel to the left, engage forward on the outside (starboard) engine, and a sharp turn will be achieved.

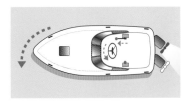

Twin shaft As with twin outdrives the outer engine has greater leverage. The engines can be used alone to effect a turn, one driving ahead and the other astern.

Twin engines or shafts make a craft far easier to control, however, on smaller craft, where the engines are less than 1m apart, the effect of twin engines is lessened. Where they are placed further apart they have more leverage, and both engines can be manipulated to steer the craft.

Turning single shaft

A single shaft drive boat is turned using bursts of ahead and astern applied when the wheel is turned hard over, so that the rudder deflects the burst of prop-wash straight away and its power is transmitted into the turn and not into forward progress. Typically a burst is 2 seconds, depending on conditions.

- Position the boat in the centre of the space. Start too close to one side and the stern may be in danger of clipping the pontoon.

- Approach slowly, speed carried into a turn makes the turning circle larger.

- Turn in the direction that the astern prop walk will aid the turn.

- Wheel hard over and give a burst ahead. Engage neutral.

- When the rate of turn slows or space ahead is limited, go astern. Changes in rudder position are ineffective as there is insufficient space to gain steerageway. Momentum and prop walk are now turning the boat.

- Once the correct direction is achieved, straighten the wheel. Select ahead.

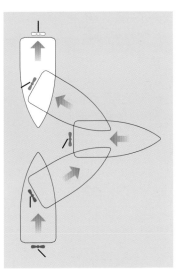

Turning a single outdrive or outboard

Turning with outdrives requires constant use of the wheel, because the wheel controls the direction of the prop wash. To achieve the tightest turn, the wheel should be turned before the prop is engaged so that valuable turning space is not used up driving the boat forward. Wash from the prop driving astern is directional and is also used to help the turn.

The order:
Neutral – turn wheel – ahead – neutral – reverse wheel – astern. Repeat the sequence until the turn is completed.

In all cases, the pivot point on outdrive boats is further back when going astern. This has the effect of making the bow drift very quickly in wind when reversing. If the bow does start drifting uncontrollably, let it and the stern will seek the wind. Reverse into the wind to make more spaces and then recover the manoeuvre by motoring forward.

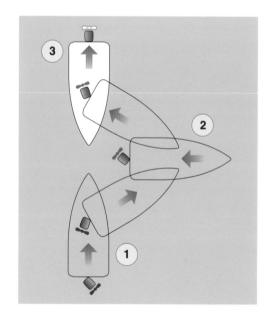

1 Motor slowly into the space.
  Stop.
  Wheel hard over to starboard.
  Engage ahead.
  Monitor the turn.
  Neutral when space is short.

2 Wheel hard over to port.
  Engage astern.
  Monitor turn.
  Neutral when space is short.

3 Straighten using wheel.
  Engage ahead.

Tip - The golden rule when boat handling in close quarters is to turn the wheel first, then apply the gear. This immediately diverts the prop wash or thrust in the correct direction.

Tip - If it all goes wrong, put the engine into neutral and fend off. Do not power out of the problem. Think it through and remember to have an escape route planned.

Turning a twin outdrive or outboard

- Use opposite wheel lock to engine, wheel to right (starboard), use left (port) engine.
- Remember pivot points move further aft in astern.
- Change wheel position between motoring ahead and astern.

1 Motor slowly into the space.
Stop.
Wheel hard over to starboard.
Ahead port engine.
Monitor the turn.
Neutral when space is short.

2 Wheel hard over to port.
Astern starboard engine.
Monitor turn.
Neutral when space is short.

3 Wheel hard over to starboard.
Ahead port engine.
Monitor turn.
Straighten helm when turn is completed.

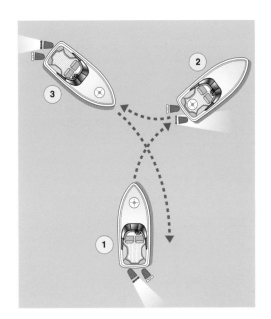

Turning a twin screw boat

Twin screw boats are very manoeuvrable because each propeller is positioned to make the most of the pivot point. A tight turn is achieved using both throttles simultaneously. Using port engine ahead and starboard engine astern twists the boat around in her own length. Using both engines combined with the wheel to starboard creates the smallest turn as the rudder diverts the prop wash from the port engine. It may be easier to start by using one engine at a time, then move on to simultaneous use.

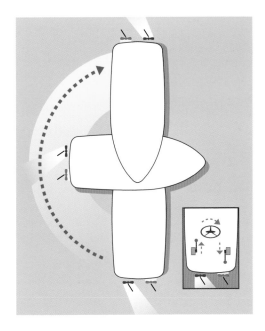

Slide

Controlling a boat is a little like controlling a car on an icy road, they both slide or drift. Turn to starboard and the boat will slide out of the turn to port because it has little grip on the water's surface. A turn at greater speed increases the slide. Try not to start a turn too late as the slide may well take you towards other vessels.

Turning in elements

When turning a boat with either wind or stream it is usual to turn towards the strongest element (for a motor boat usually the wind) especially in a confined space. Once the bow is through the element the wind or stream will help push the bow in the desired direction. It is very important to keep an eye on the wind and stream direction and watch out for slide and drift on your approach.

- Wheel hard over.
- Engage Ahead.

  When the bow is into or through the wind:

- Engage neutral and reverse the wheel.
- Go astern.

  When the boat is pointing in the correct direction:

- Engage neutral.
- Reverse the wheel and go ahead.

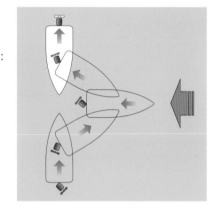

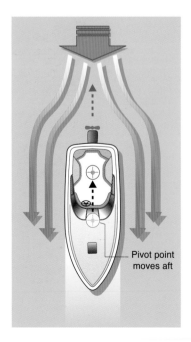

Pivot point moves aft

Remember

- The wind may help the turn but may blow you towards other craft, so leave enough space.
- Wheel first - then power.
- Pivot point moves aft in astern.
- Outdrive boats are very light at the bow and you will lose the bow very quickly in a strong breeze.
- A bow-thruster can make the turn easier but many are not powerful enough to push the bow through the wind.

Tip - If the elements take over; the bow will disappear downwind quite rapidly. Let it, and then reverse away as the stern will seek the wind.

Leaving and Coming Alongside

Leaving a pontoon or berth

Coming away from a pontoon is a relatively simple manoeuvre. If the route ahead is clear and there is no wind or stream, then for small boats a good push off the pontoon and driving away forward can do the trick. However, larger craft require you to drive it off.

Coming away in reverse is often the best way to leave a berth.

- Steer away from the pontoon.

- Engage reverse.

- As the stern comes away straighten up the wheel.

- Once well clear move off ahead.

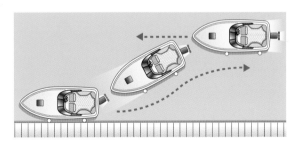

As boats are more curved at the bow than the stern it is possible to fender the bow area well and motor gently towards the pontoon for a second to push the stern away from the pontoon. This creates space for the stern to reverse clear.
This is especially true for single shaft drive craft.

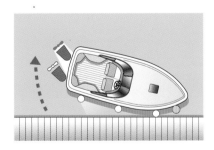

Twin outdrives

Here is a case for not using opposite helm and engine. Turn the helm to the left and put the left engine in astern. This tends to lift the boat from the dock.

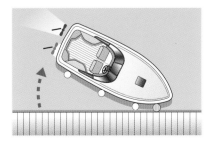

Twin shafts

Protect the bow with fenders and go astern on the inside prop. If there is an onshore wind you might need to turn the helm towards the dock and use a touch of ahead from the outside prop or use a bow line to pull against.

Using a line to assist leaving a berth

If the wind is pushing the boat onto the pontoon, or if the berth is restricted, motoring against a line can allow the stern to get into clear water and allow an easy exit.

Reversing on a bow line

- Rig up a bow slip line.
- Fender the bow well.
- Steer away from the dock.
- Engage astern.
- The stern starts to pivot away from the pontoon into clear water.
- Engage neutral.
- Slip the bow line and reverse away.

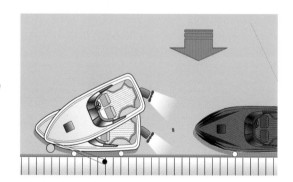

This works well for all craft with the exception of single shaft drive. On twin engine vessels use the engine nearest the pontoon.

Bow spring line

- Rig a bow spring line and fender the bow area.
- Motor forwards to bring the bow in and the stern away from the pontoon.
- Engage Neutral.
- Slip the spring and reverse away.

This works well for single engined craft.

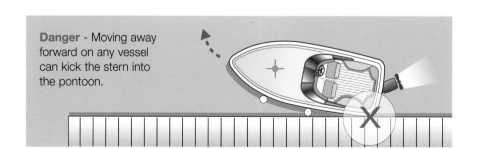

Danger - Moving away forward on any vessel can kick the stern into the pontoon.

Coming alongside

Tight manoeuvring among pontoons and other boats can be made far easier and less stressful with planning and preparation, and by taking into account how the wind and stream will affect the boat. Before approaching:

- Consider what the wind and stream are doing. How will they affect your approach? Approaching into the wind or stream will act as a brake to the boat. Ideally, approach into whichever will have the greatest effect.

- Brief your crew so they know exactly what is expected of them.

- Prepare fenders and lines.

- Plan your 'escape' route, in case the plan goes wrong.

The idea is to berth the boat in one flowing movement and with practice this can be achieved.

The process can also be broken down into smaller steps to make it easier to understand.

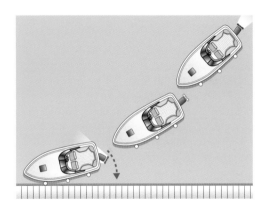

1 Start your approach as far off the pontoon as is practical. Your angle of approach should be about 30°–40°. Keep speed to a minimum by using neutral.

2 When close, steer away from the pontoon and engage forward gear momentarily to bring the boat alongside. Ideally, you should glide to a stop alongside the pontoon. Be prepared to go astern to stop.

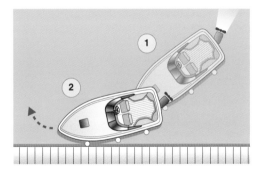

3 You can also slow the boat and bring the stern in by turning the wheel towards the dock and applying astern momentarily.

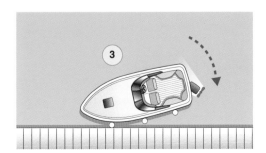

Wind off pontoon

Just as we have used lines to help us leave a berth, we can also use them to help us get alongside. These techniques are especially useful if the wind is blowing the boat away from the pontoon.

1 Attach a bow line to a cleat on the pontoon (lassoing the cleat is the easiest method – see page 71).

2 Turn the steering wheel towards the pontoon. Engage reverse at tick-over/idle.

3 Craft moves slowly alongside. Attach stern line and take out of gear.

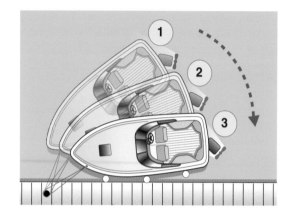

In certain circumstances and particluarly in craft with a high free board and lots of windage or poor bow access, it can be easier to let the stern seek the wind and reverse towards the pontoon.

1 Fender the stern well and watch out for bathing platforms (if fitted).

2 From within the safety of the cockpit area; the crew lasso the stern cleat with the stern line, leaving 1-2m of line between the stern and the pontoon.

3 Steer towards the pontoon and engage forward at tick-over speed. The boat is then 'driven' alongside the pontoon.

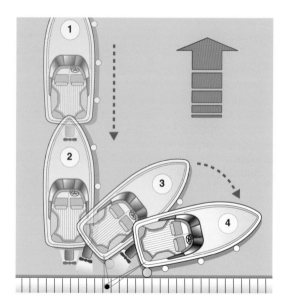

Twin engine

Using one engine at a time, motor slowly towards the pontoon. When the cleat is near the bow, stop the boat, lasso the cleat with the bow line, take up any slack and secure. Engage tick-over astern on the outside engine. This pulls back on the bow line and pivots the stern towards the pontoon. When the stern is close to the pontoon, secure.

Mooring in a marina

Coming into a marina berth requires extra care because there are moored boats and vessels moving around.

If you are visiting, call the marina office on your VHF to establish which side to put your fenders out. 'Starboard-side-to' means your lines and fenders will be placed on the right if you enter the berth facing forwards.

Consider these marina berths:

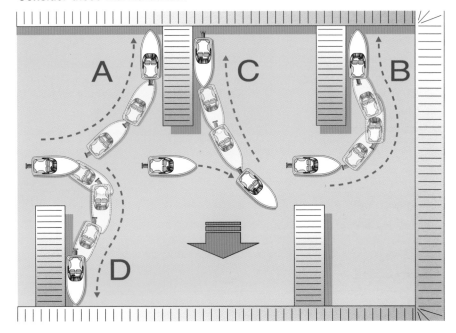

A Approaching into wind this will naturally slow the boat. The momentum of the boat will help it slide sideways alongside the berth.

B The turning momentum will tend to slide the boat away from the berth.

C As the stern seeks the wind in astern, this boat reverses easily into the berth.

D The wind will push the craft into the berth, so care is needed not to overshoot. Put a stern line on early.

Mooring in wind and stream

Ferry gliding

It is possible to drift a boat sideways by steering into the elements using gentle throttle turning the boat slightly so that the wind or stream is pushing on one side of the bow, thus enabling you to 'crab' sideways in that direction. This is called ferry gliding and it can be used to come alongside pontoons or other boats in a slow, controlled manner.

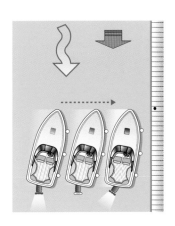

Special Moorings

Pen moorings

Piles can also be used to keep a boat off the dock in a mooring pen. Lines are attached to the dock and the two stern lines, connected to the piles, hold the boat away.

Rig up two bow lines and two stern lines.

Lead the windward stern line to the beam.

The windward lines are attached first to stop the boat drifting.

Depending on the space between the piles, fenders may or may not be used.

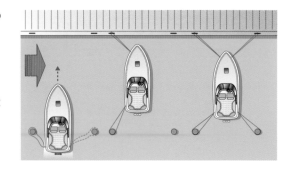

Motor towards the windward pile and place a stern line over the pile. Do the same with the leeward pile if time and crew strength permit.

Motor forwards and attach the bow lines, windward line first.

Position the boat by easing the bow and pulling in on the stern.

Sometimes one of the piles is replaced by a pontoon for ease of access to the shore. This allows the boat to be held away from the pontoon by tightening up on the pile line and the corresponding line astern. Pick up lines are usually supplied on the piles to aid retrieval.

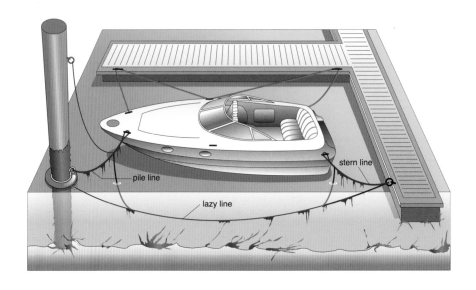

pile line

stern line

lazy line

Stern-to and bows-to mooring

Mooring outside the UK is usually stern or bows to the quay. Motorboats usually moor stern to the quay for ease of access to the shore. Stern lines are used to stay close to the quay, while the anchor holds the boat away. A passerelle or wooden plank, carried by the boat, is used to go ashore.

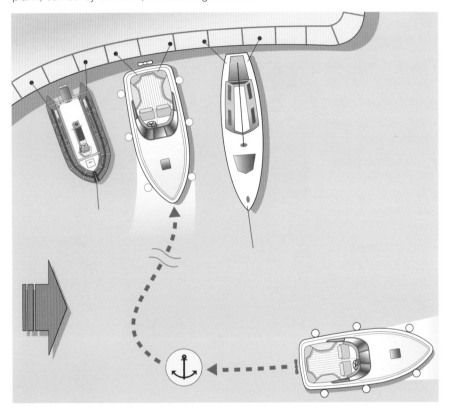

The approach

- Rig up fenders on both sides and a large fender on the stern. Rig stern lines from both quarters.

- Prepare to drop the anchor.

- Reverse towards the wind.

- Four boat lengths away from the quay drop the anchor and ease out chain.

- One boat length from the quay, stop easing the chain so that the anchor digs in. Be ready to let out more chain if required.

- Connect the windward stern line to the shore, followed by the leeward stern line.

- Once positioned the correct distance from the quay, take the strain up on the chain.

Bows-to mooring

It is also possible to drop a kedge (stern) anchor and moor up bows-to the quay. Use two bow lines to attach to the quay wall and bridle the kedge anchor warp to centre the stern.

Lazy lines

Lazy lines are used in tight harbours and marinas where it is unsuitable to drop the anchor because it may become fouled. Instead of an anchor holding the bow away, the bow is connected to a heavy bow line, which is attached to a concrete block. The bow line is also attached to a lighter line, which is led to the quayside for ease of retrieval.

The approach

- Rig up fenders either side and at the stern.

- Rig two stern lines.

- Reverse towards the quay.

- Connect windward stern line to quay.

- Pick up lazy line, lead to bow and tie off.

- Connect second stern line.

- Adjust bow and stern lines.

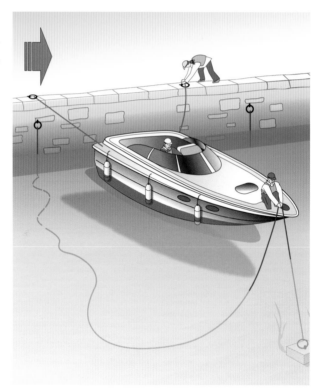

It is possible to hold the boat in position once the windward stern line is attached by applying small nudges ahead on the leeward engine.

Tip - If it is safe to do so, have a crew member forward with a roving fender ready to fend off from craft adjacent to you.

In very windy or a difficult berth consider dropping a crew member off to tend lines for you, or if short handed call the marina for assistance.

Mooring buoys

Picking up a mooring buoy

Mooring buoys are laid by individuals and harbour authorities for permanent moorings and visitors. Most visitors' buoys have markings and in some areas their position is noted on a chart or pilot book.

Buoys vary; some have obvious rings on top and others have chain loops hanging from below attached via a line to the pick up buoy. Never tie off to the pick up buoy.

Before picking up a mooring buoy consider:

- Check there is sufficient depth now and for the duration of your stay.

- Ensure it will give shelter from the present and forecast wind.

- Head into the wind or stream so that it acts as a brake.

- Pick up buoys float downstream and are a good indication of stream direction.

- Sailing boats and powerboats often sit in different directions with wind and stream. Sailing yachts have a keel and this is affected more by stream than wind. Powerboats have little grip on the water and tend to lay with the wind.

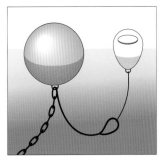

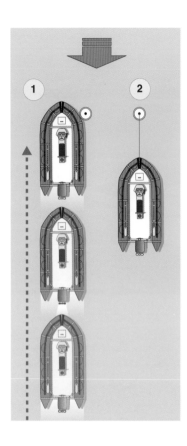

- To approach the buoy, start your run from downwind or stream. Alternate between neutral and tick-over forward so your approach is slow and controlled.

- Judge your speed by looking sideways at passing objects.

- You require the minimum of speed while still having full control.

- If you do overshoot, go into neutral to avoid tangling the mooring in the prop.

- If mooring to a buoy with a ring use at least two turns around the ring as the movement with chafe through the line.

- If using a pick-up buoy ensure that you connect to the heavy line attached to it and not the light line on the buoy itself.

- With some craft, where it is difficult to pick up a mooring buoy from the foredeck, consider approaching astern.

- Rig a line from a forward cleat back to the cockpit area.

- Reverse up to the buoy.

- Tie off as described above.

- The vessel will then swing round.

- For a short stay a stern line can be used.

Tip - If you are moored to someone else's mooring buoy, a crew member must stay with the boat and be prepared to move it should the owners return.

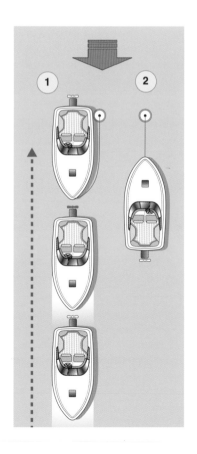

Anchoring

Anchoring allows you to stop for lunch or overnight in quiet and pleasant surroundings away from the crowds. It is also the first line of action if the engine fails in shallow water because it stops the boat and allows the problem to be resolved.

There are various types of anchors. The choice depends on your chosen cruising ground. Some anchors have good holding in mud and sand, others are designed to pierce weed and get in between rocks.

CQR or Plough

A strong anchor with good holding power.

Danforth

A flat anchor with good holding, always lies flat.

Bruce

A good anchor with excellent holding.

Delta

Almost a fixed version of the Plough (without the hinge) often used by craft with electric anchor winches, as it resets itself well into the bow roller.

All of these anchors have good holding in a variety of surfaces. The one best suited to your needs is dependent on your boat type, the area you will be anchoring in, and how easy each will be to stow. Other anchors include:

Grapnell

Poor holding versus recommended anchors.

Fishermans

Awkward to stow and heavier than other anchors of similar holding power.

Mud anchor

Not often used by small sports boats but useful for river craft.

Things to consider before anchoring include:

- Look for a sheltered anchorage, consider wind direction later.
- Take a trial run to assess depth.
- Avoid main channels and submarine power lines; use charts to identify areas.
- Prepare the anchor line and anchor.
- How much rope needs to be put out?
- Check charts for obstructions and what ground to expect.

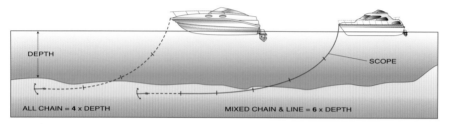

The anchor is connected to a 'scope' of chain, or a chain and rope combination. The amount of scope let out when anchoring depends on whether the scope is all chain or a mixture. The more scope you let out reduces the chances of the boat snatching the anchor out of the seabed. It also acts as a shock absorber.

The amount of scope carried on board depends on your area of operation. In shallow estuaries 30m would be sufficient whereas in deep and rocky areas considerably more may be required.

It is usual to have two anchors on board; a main anchor and a smaller kedge anchor. Both should have their own warp or chain.

Dropping the anchor

The process of anchoring is very similar to picking up a mooring buoy. RIBs and speedboats with open bows are easier to anchor, because going forward is easy. On larger craft with anchor lockers at the bow, a crew member must go onto the foredeck to anchor but with caution, keeping their centre of gravity low.

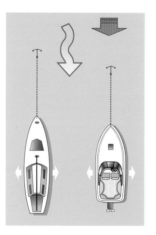

- Look for shelter.
- Check depth.
- Motor into the strongest element.
- When at the chosen point stop the boat.
- Drop the anchor to the seabed.
- As vessel drifts back, ease out scope to 4:1 (all chain) or 6:1 (rope chain) ratio.
- Make fast and engage reverse briefly to dig the anchor in.

Dragging and swinging

Yachts and powerboats move in different ways as the stream or wind changes.

Check your anchor is not dragging by:

- Identifying a transit and checking it at regular intervals.
- Setting up the anchor-drag function on your GPS.
- Taking a bearing from a hand bearing compass.

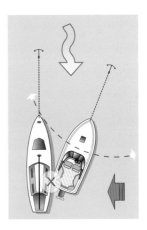

- If your anchor is dragging, you will need to raise it and re-anchor.

- If it continues to drag choose a different anchorage.

- If the objects in transit cease to be lined up or the bearing changes, you are dragging.

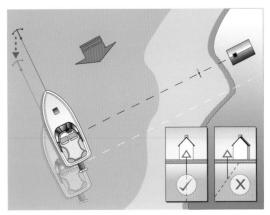

Raising the anchor

- Check to see how the boat is lying.
- If the boat is pulling back away from the anchor, you may need to slowly motor towards the anchor as the crew pulls in the slack and raises the anchor.
- Good crew communication is essential to avoid overrunning and fouling the prop.
- Hand signals between crew and helmsman are useful.
- Bring the anchor and line on-board, and stow it away so it is ready for immediate redeployment.

Tip - Anchors stored in the bow lockers may do considerable damage if not secured.

Make sure your anchor line is suitable. Nylon is good, it is elastic and it does not float.

9 | Travelling at Speed

If your vessel is fitted with a kill cord it is safest to wear it at all times. At speed ensure that your crew have a good seating position, a firm grip, and know what you are going to do before you do it. They can only know what you are going to do if you tell them beforehand.

Avoid situations which involve rapid changes in direction. Take early action in potential collision situations and remember, if in doubt, take the power off reducing the closing speeds of vessels. Keep a good look out for other craft, keep a watch for and predict the effect of waves or the wash from other vessels. By keeping alert and assessing situations early, you can make high speed driving safe and fun.

Travelling at high speed

It takes a lot of power to get on the plane. Once there it may be necessary to throttle back slightly to ease speed and conserve fuel. A displacement or semi-displacement hull will never achieve the ability to plane on the top of the water so its speed will be governed by hull form and the power available.

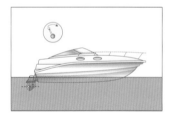
Before moving away, ensure that the engine is 'trimmed in' to ensure that it is pushed flush against the stern of the boat; this helps the boat get up onto the "plane".

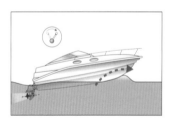
As the throttle is pushed forward a powerboat begins to move from being a displacement boat at low speed and starts to climb on top of her bow wave and get on the "plane".

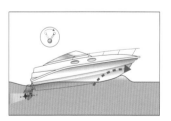
As speed increases, less of the boat is touching the water. This reduces friction allowing speed to to be maintained with less power.

High speed turns

Whenever turning at speed it is important to warn the crew so that they are not thrown out of the boat. Turning too sharply allows the prop to suck in air (ventilate) and loose grip on the water. Slowing the rate of turn or the amount of revs will allow the prop to grip again. Trim down before commencing a turn for greater grip and control during the turn.

Turns through 180°

When approaching a turn; set up the boat by trimming-in the leg, take off some speed, look around especially behind, warn your crew, then execute a wide turn keeping the boat on the plane by managing the throttle. If you turn too tightly most of the speed will be lost. Coming out of the turn apply power and trim-out.

S-turns

S-turns (gradual turns to the right or left) can be made at reasonably high speed as long as they are steady and controlled, when the conditions are suitable.

Power Trim

An outdrive leg or outboard can be trimmed in or out to change the angle of the propeller's thrust. This changes the fore and aft trim of the boat. Trim affects comfort, fuel consumption and handling characteristics, especially in heavy weather.

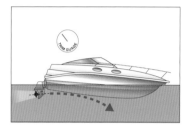

Leg in to start to keep the prop in the water and help the boat get on the plane.

On the plane ease the leg out to achieve the best speed. Ease out too much and the prop sucks in air from the surface, making it spin faster but lose grip on the water, therefore slowing the boat. Ease the leg out by the correct amount and the revs increase slightly without the throttle being adjusted, therefore speed increases.

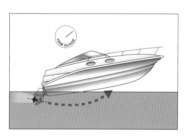

If the boat starts to porpoise (the bow bounces up and down), trim the leg in to regain control, then slowly ease out to re-trim.

Trim needs constant adjustment. If crew move around the boat or there is a change in sea conditions or speed, you need to check the trim. Fuel use makes the boat lighter – you will need to trim between full and half tanks.

Tip - Even when trim gauges are fitted, they can be unreliable. Practise in various conditions to get the best trim. When there are no gauges, use time increments to know whether the leg is up, down or centred. When trimmed correctly the revs rise slightly and the helm feels lighter without pull to either side.

Trim tabs

Trim tabs are either flat plates or vertical blades fitted either side of the boat and attached to the transom. They are used to trim or level the boat, both fore and aft and side to side.

Trim tabs are controlled up and downwards by either a hydraulic, or electric ram system on the transom.

- Tabs down – raises the stern which in turn depresses the bow (bow down).

- Tabs up – lowers the stern which in turn raises the bow (bow up).

- As a basic rule you tab down into a head-sea and tab up with a following sea.

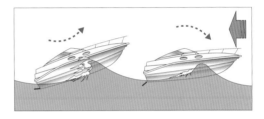

- Tabs can also be used to compensate for a beam sea or uneven loading.

- One tab down – raises one side of the boat. This is useful to compensate for loading irregularities or a beam sea.

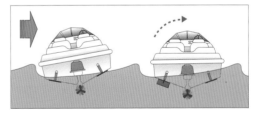

Gauges are rarely fitted to advise you how much trim is used. While in port count how long the tabs take to rise, lower and centre, then use time increments for their positioning.

Tabs can be helpful when getting up on the plane. Tab down to lift the stern. Tabs should not be needed, but may help compensate for the crew standing at the rear or weed on the hull.

Although tabs are mainly used at speed, they can also be used tabbed down in marinas to increase grip on the water. Beware of powerful reversing when tabbed down, as this can cause damage to the tabs.

Tabs make a huge difference to comfort and sea-keeping ability at speed. It is possible to achieve basic steering using one tab at a time.

Experimentation in different conditions will give the best compromise of comfort, fuel consumption and ride, but tab half down is a good starting point.

10 | Difficult Conditions

At some stage everyone faces conditions at sea which test both their boat and self. Knowing what to do in these situations makes all the difference.

In rough conditions, try to match your speed and direction to the conditions by careful control of the throttles and steering. Jumping from wave to wave or ploughing through waves can be great fun, but yourself, crew and boat will find it very wearing. Make sure that everyone has good handholds and seating positions and the helmsman is wearing the kill-cord.

Driving upwind

Waves are generally generated by wind and come from the same direction. Driving into the wind therefore means driving into the waves. Driving downwind the boat drives with the waves, applying special techniques will ensure safety and comfort.

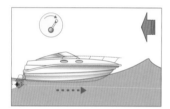

Driving upwind usually entails trimming down and driving up the face of the wave.

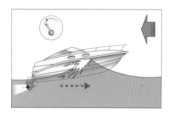

Ease off at the top of the wave to ensure you do not take off.

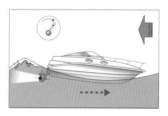

Accelerate down the back of the wave, speeding up to raise the bow as the trough is reached, then drive up the wave towards the next crest.

The ride then becomes smooth and quite fast. Progression is achieved by throttling on and off as you move over the wave. Trimming down ensures that the 'V' of the hull is used to slice into the approaching wave, while applying more throttle lifts the bow in the trough to drive up the approaching wave and prevent the bow driving straight into it. This avoids the need for trimming up and down to achieve the same affect.

> **Tip** - Upwind - This can be summed up as: when the bow is rising - throttle back, when the bow is falling - throttle up.

Whether this proves to be a comfortable ride depends to a large extent on the 'wavelength' (the distance between the wave crests). Shorter wavelengths can make it very difficult, as there is little time between wave crests for the helmsman to adjust the throttle settings. In this case, you might find it easier to drive at 30°–45° to the wave front. This increases the 'apparent wavelength' and can therefore allow you to increase your speed and smooth your journey. You will then need to zigzag towards your destination but, while longer in distance, this method can be less stressful and quicker.

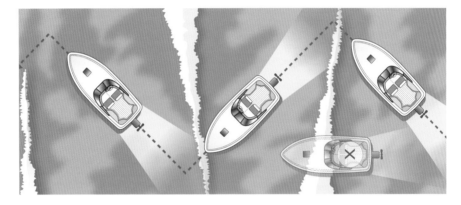

Beam seas

Large breaking waves taken on the beam have the potential to capsize a boat. Usually keep a fair speed, constantly watch for breaking waves, then steer a path behind, or in front of and away from them, as conditions dictate. The speed and power of your boat is key. If you get caught on the downwind side of a breaking wave, turn into the wave and power on to climb up the wave or turn away from the wave and try to outrun it.

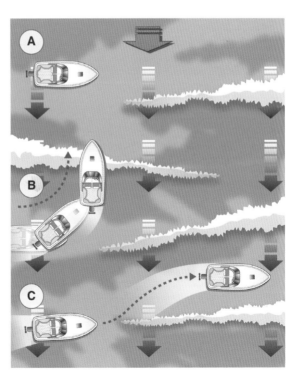

Driving downwind

One of the most dangerous conditions for a sportsboat is a 'following sea' (the craft is running in the direction of the wind). If a breaking wave catches the vessel, the confused water catches the prop, reducing its ability to bite. The following wave then turns the craft side on to the waves making a capsize almost inevitable with the next wave. To avoid this, match the boat's speed to that of the waves. Another problem of going down the face of a wave is going too fast through the wave causing the bow to fall into the trough. The boat loses speed, the wave pivots the boat beam on and either swamps or capsizes the boat.

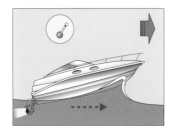

To make progress in these conditions, trim the bow up and ride the wave, staying behind the the crest.

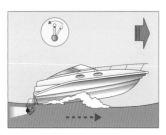

As it breaks, care is needed not to power through the breaking wave too early. As the wave breaks, you may need to ease the power in the confused water to avoid the prop losing grip and speed. A good look out must be kept behind at all times to avoid the chasing waves catching you up. Alternatively, pick a calm patch to turn into the sea and look for another port.

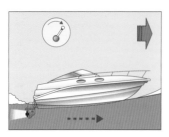

Watch the boat speed as you may need to ease the throttle, then power through to sit on the back of the next wave.

The conditions you experience may be magnified or reduced by the combination of wind, stream and the local environment. Wind in the opposite direction to the stream ('wind against stream') can create short, sharp and unpleasant seas when driving upwind, yet markedly different conditions if driving downwind. Short, sharp seas can be difficult to deal with, as the helmsman has little time between each wave to recover and plan how to deal with the next one.

Harbour bar

When a large following sea is found at the entrance to a harbour, the conditions can get even livelier and generally should not be attempted. As the depth of water near land reduces the waves grow in height, break earlier and more violently and the change in conditions can be dramatic.

Search Patterns

As you become more experienced, you may venture further off the beaten track and sometimes be caught out in less than perfect sea conditions. This increases the chance of you becoming involved in incidents requiring conducting a search or taking part in a helicopter transfer. Prior knowledge of what you and your crew should do will be a great advantage.

Search patterns

A search pattern could be used to find a crew member who has fallen overboard or to look for a person or boat that has been reported in the area. If you need to undertake a search, there are a number of considerations:

- Ensure the rescue authorities are aware of the situation. They will task SAR (Search and Rescue) resources to assist.

- If you have lost someone overboard, you should start your search in the area in which they are now most likely to be. They may have drifted some distance. The starting point is known as the 'datum' point.

It is important that the search efficiently covers the search area. It should also be simple enough for the crew to execute effectively. The simplest effective search is the 'expanding box search'.

Expanding Box Search

- 'D' is the 'Detection range' and is the maximum distance at which an observer in the boat can see a casualty in the water for half the time. A fender or similar object may be used to calculate this range.

- The length of the leg grows every two legs.

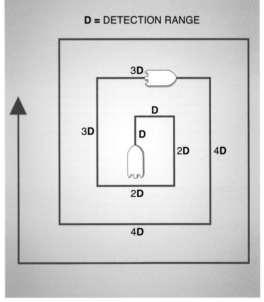

- The direction of the initial leg is in the direction the casualty is most likely to have drifted, (although many people start north up as it keeps it simple) and each turn is 90° to starboard.

Learning how to execute a search pattern should never be left until you have to do it. Find a suitable area of water, drop an item into the water and practise retrieving it with your regular crew.

12 | Man Overboard

A person falling overboard (MOB) is a serious situation, therefore:

If someone goes overboard

- Alert the crew by shouting 'Man overboard'.
- Instruct one person to point at the MOB at all times.
- At slow speed turn the wheel towards the MOB. This moves the prop away from the MOB.
- Effect a slow controlled turn back towards the MOB.
- A MOB is a Mayday or a DSC alert.

Recovery

Return to and recovery of the MOB is the most important element. Make sure you know which recovery method best suits your boat and crew. Muscles lose their strength very quickly in cold water so do not expect much help from the MOB. Practice just in case you have to do it for real one day. Below are two recovery techniques:

Method 1 – into the wind

- Give plenty of room and approach from downwind.
- Reduce power, then move slowly towards the MOB.
- Use neutral to control your speed.
- Keep the MOB on the windward bow.
- When close enough, remove all power and grab hold of the MOB.
- Switch off the engine*.
- Assist the MOB to an area of the boat where they can be recovered.

Advantages

- Suits smaller craft with low freeboards.
- Allows waves to be taken head-on.
- Good when rough as MOB is unlikely to go under the boat.

Disadvantages

- Need to be prompt at collection time.
- Can lose sight of MOB under the bow.
- Can be difficult if alone in boat.

*As skipper you need to balance switching off the engine for the safety of the MOB against the experience of the helm and the sea conditions you are facing.

Method 2 – Beam on approach

- Drive upwind of the MOB.

- Stop and position upwind of MOB.

- Slowly adjust position to drift down onto the MOB.

- When alongside switch off engine*.

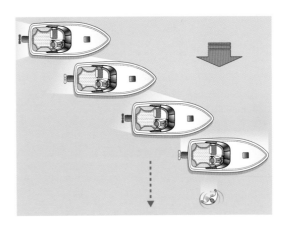

Advantages

- Suits high-bowed vessels where sight of the MOB is easily lost while approaching them into the wind.

- Greater collection area - whole side of the vessel.

- Provides some shelter to MOB. Allows boat to be easily brought alongside MOB by cockpit area, where freeboard is lowest.

The Williamson turn

If it is night or poor light you may need to use the Williamson turn to return to the MOB. This requires a compass orientated turn to return back to the MOB. First alter your heading either way by 60° then reverse the turn onto the reciprocal of your original heading. The MOB should be in front of you as you are travelling the reciprocal of your original heading.

Disadvantages

- Can be uncomfortable beam onto sea.

- Small craft can be blown over the MOB.

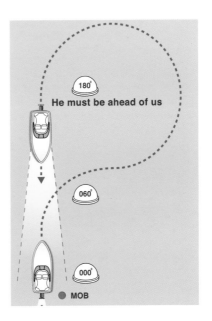

Causes and prevention

- At slow speed, sharp throttle movements can catch people unaware. Brief crew before speeding up and ensure they hold on.

- At higher speed, ensure crew are seated and holding on. Beware of sudden wheel movements.

- Young children need full time supervision.

- Cover this in your safety briefing.

13 | Helicopter Rescue

If you or your crew require emergency evacuation a helicopter may be sent to your assistance. It is most likely that a helicopter crew will seek to undertake a 'high-line' transfer but helicopter procedures do differ from country to country.

- Before the helicopter arrives, prepare your boat for its arrival and secure all loose items

- The helicopter pilot will make contact by VHF and give a brief on what is going to happen. Small Craft are usually attended with the boat stationary, however the brief may give a course and speed you should follow. Listen very carefully and take notes.

- If asked to steer a course and speed it is important to keep to it without deviating.

- A weighted line is lowered. Let it earth in the water to release any static. Do not attach it to the boat. Pull on the line to guide the helicopter winch-man to the boat. Gloves are useful.

- Coil the line; a bucket is useful.

- The winch-man will land on deck, unhook and assess the situation. He now has complete authority.

- If the casualty needs to be removed from the boat the winch-man will take the casualty off the boat. You will use the weighted line to control his swing. Do not let it snag on anything.

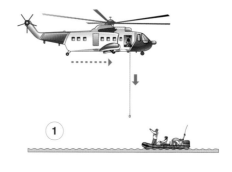

1

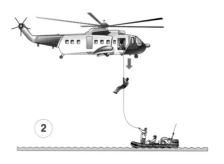

2

3

4

Towing on the Water

Good seamanship dictates that you should come to the aid of a boater in distress or needing assistance. Often this amounts to the request for a tow from a stricken powerboat or yacht.

There are two ways of towing

Long tow The towed craft is attached on a long line to your own. This is suitable in areas of open water away from other craft.

Alongside tow When you are close to other craft (perhaps entering a marina), or a confined river where greater control of the towed craft is required.

Long tow

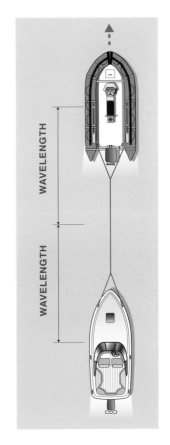

- Use the longest line practical as it acts as a shock absorber between tug and tow and reduces the strain on fittings.

- Form a short bridle around your transom. Doing this utilises the strongest points, spreads the load and centres the pull.

- The disabled vessel should either tie the tug's line to their D-ring on the bow, if fitted, or onto a bridle led from their two forward cleats.

- The length of the line should allow the vessels to be twice the distance between wave crests or troughs, this ensures that both boats ride the waves together, and reduces snatching.

- Snatching can be reduced by hanging a weight, such as an anchor, from the centre of the towline.

- The helm of the towed craft can steer to help the tug.

- If the towed craft is veering around as it is being towed, ask the skipper to move the weight aft or drag warps etc to give the stern drag and stability.

- Stay clear of main shipping lanes and channels.

- Inform the Coastgaurd.

The speed of the tow will be determined by the sea state and the power of the towing craft. Maintaining a low speed of 5–8 knots is best and reduces strain on both craft.

Side tow

The key to a successful side tow is correctly setting up the position of the craft relative to each other and ensuring that suitable lines are rigged between them.

Key points are:

- Fender the boats well.

- The rudder or engine of the towing vessel should be set well behind the stern of the towed craft.

- The towed craft should be angled slightly into the towing vessel.

- The spring line between the bow of the towing vessel and the stern of the disabled craft takes about 100% of the strain when towing forward. The spring from the rear of the towing vessel to the bow of the disabled craft does so when towing in reverse.

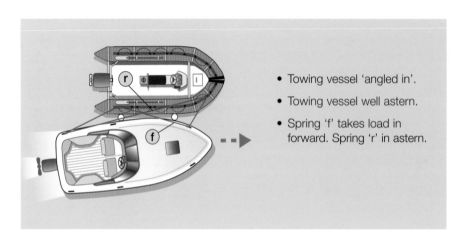

- Towing vessel 'angled in'.

- Towing vessel well astern.

- Spring 'f' takes load in forward. Spring 'r' in astern.

Being towed.

If you need a tow, ensure:

- The tow craft is capable of the tow - a 12ft speedboat might be keen to practise towing on your 25ft cruiser, but is it safe?

- **Salvage** Agree a price at the outset for fuel or a few beers once at the slipway. It's also good practice to offer them a line you have prepared as evidence that you retain control of your vessel.

Manoeuvring

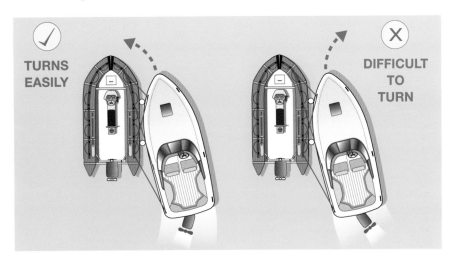

The two tied vessels have distinct handling characteristics. Once you understand these, precise towing is quite straightforward. Think of the set-up as a twin-engined craft with only one engine working. The outside engine on the turn has the greatest leverage.

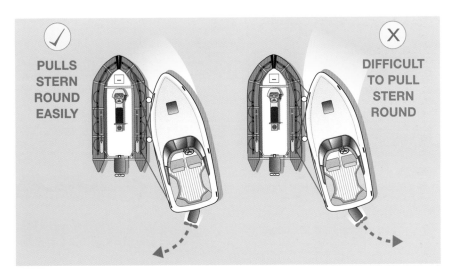

Turns easily = small turning circle.   Difficult to turn = large turning circle.

Tip - Before commencing a tow you should consider whether you and your boat are capable of the tow. Your first responsibility has to be to your own crew. Taking on a tow beyond your and your boat's capability would be foolhardy. Call for professional assistance if necessary.

15 | Knots and Rope Work

You do not need to know how to tie a large number of knots, but make sure you can tie a few knots well.

Bowline

This is probably the most useful knot to be able to tie, and has a variety of uses:

- The loop can easily be draped over a bollard, tow ball or cleat.

- Two bow lines can be easily tied together joining two lines.

It can take a very high load, but cannot be untied under load.

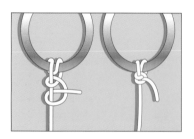

Round turn and two half-hitches

This is useful for tasks such as tying to a mooring buoy or ring. It is also very useful for tying fenders on to rails, and tying covers down tightly.

One of the key benefits of the knot is that once the turn is on, the knot can be tied and untied while under load.

Clove hitch

Generally used for tying fenders on. Also used to tie on to bollards or car tow hitches.

This knot should only be used under low loads as it can jam and be hard to undo.

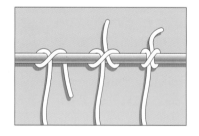

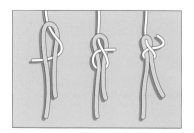

Sheet bend

This is useful for joining two ropes together as, for example, to extend a mooring line.

Taking a turn and tying to a cleat

Because large loads come onto a warp, keep fingers a safe distance away from the cleat.

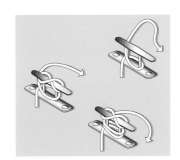

Take a full turn around the cleat – this takes the load of the boat whilst still allowing the warp to be eased or taken in.

A figure of eight takes more strain, then two more turns complete the sequence – the boat is now secure and the cleat may be left.

Coiling and stowing a line

Open your left palm and lay equal sized coils into it. As each coil is laid, turn the line between your thumb and forefinger clockwise. This has the effect of creating neat coils. Finish off by wrapping the line around the coil. Thread the end through the coil to secure.

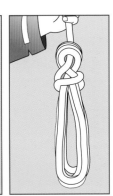

Throwing a rope

Coil the line as described above. Separate the single coil into two smaller coils. Ensure that the end of the line is secured, and then throw the coil. Allow the other coil to play out from an open palm.

Lassoing a cleat

Secure one end of the line to the cleat onboard and secure the other end by standing on it. Coil the line, then separate the coils into two smaller coils. Holding one coil in each hand, when close enough to the cleat you intend lassoing, throw both coils to land either side of the cleat.

Types of rope

3-strand nylon Has excellent stretch properties, is good for mooring, anchor lines and towing. Easy to splice. Suffers some loss of strength when wet.

3-strand polyester Many versions of polyester come 'pre-stretched'. These are not very good for anchoring or mooring. Polyester is harder wearing.

Dockline A nylon line with a harder wearing polyester cover that is generally used for mooring. Available in a variety of colours.

Anchorplait High elasticity and easy of coiling into an anchor locker make this an excellent choice for anchor lines. Is also used for mooring lines.

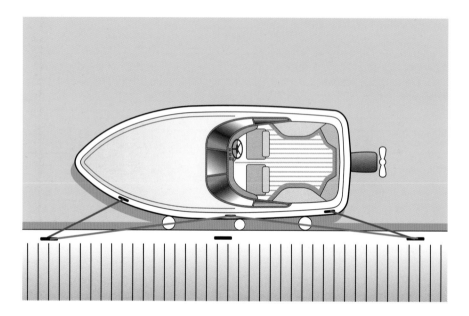

What lines should you carry?

Smaller powerboats tend to carry two main lines which are used for mooring. These should be approximately twice the length of the boat and each can be used to tie off at the bow and stern. They should be long enough to be run back to the centre of the boat as spring lines (red). 'Springs' are tied to prevent the craft moving backwards and forwards on its berth. It is good practice to carry two spare lines, both of which are twice the length of the boat.

The anchor line should be as long as possible and can double as a tow line if not spliced to the chain. Estimate the depth in places where you go boating, multiply the depth by six and buy a line of that length. In practice, a small powerboat may have an anchor line long enough for a typical anchorage plus an extra 30m line stored away in case the need arises to tow, or for emergencies.

Collision Regulations

How craft avoid each other at sea is covered by the International Regulations Preventing Collisions at Sea (IRPCS).

A skipper has a legal responsibility to follow these rules. Most are common sense, for example:

- You have a responsibility to follow the rules.

- You must keep a good lookout.

- You must avoid a collision by taking clear and obvious actions.

- Always use a safe speed.

Because powerboats are very manoeuvrable, they usually give way to all other types of craft (e.g. sailing boats, rowing boats, fishing vessels, vessels restricted in their ability to manoeuvre or not under command).

The first question is "Does a risk of collision exist?" If there is a risk, then both skippers have responsibilities. One is deemed the 'stand on' vessel and the other the 'give way' vessel. If both obey the rules this works well - however, there is no absolute right and wrong and you <u>both</u> have a duty to avoid a close quarters situation or a collision.

Common Sense

A 14ft powerboat and a supertanker at sea are governed by these rules. However discretion is the better part of valour. Common sense dictates that it is far better to keep well clear of a potential collision situation than test the larger craft's readiness to give way. The supertanker might be:
Constrained by its draught in a narrow channel and unable to turn, or the vessel may be restricted in its ability to manoeuvre, towing, trawling or dredging.

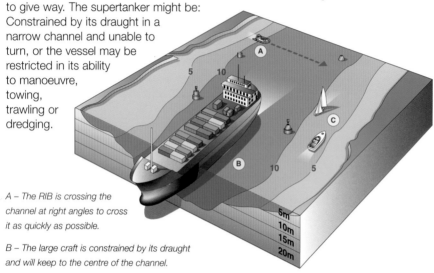

A – The RIB is crossing the channel at right angles to cross it as quickly as possible.

B – The large craft is constrained by its draught and will keep to the centre of the channel.

C – Smaller craft can keep outside the channel if there is enough depth, but still pass port to port.

How can you predict if a risk of collision exists?

If relative bearings between two vessels remain constant, a collision will occur unless action is taken to avoid it.

Irrespective of whether you are the 'give way' or 'stand on' (have right of way) vessel, you have a responsibility to avoid each other and must take every precaution to avoid a collision.

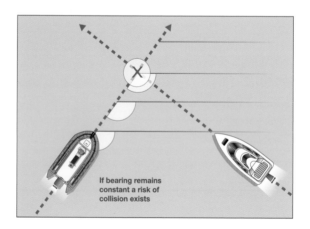

If bearing remains constant a risk of collision exists

Danger - The stand-on vessel should avoid a turn to port.

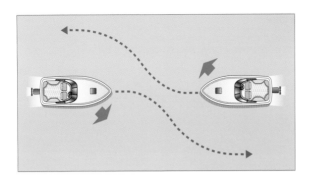

Head on

Each vessel must make a clear and obvious turn to starboard in order to pass port to port well clear of each other. If no risk of collision exists, craft can pass well clear of each other, starboard to starboard.

Crossing situation

The stand on vessel should hold its course and speed (but continue to carefully monitor what action the other vessel is taking), while the give-way vessel should alter its course and/or speed to stay clear of the other vessel.

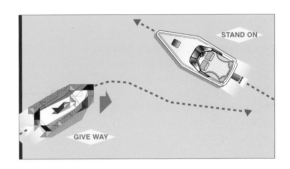

Give way or stand-on?

- You are the give way vessel in a crossing situation if you see the other craft approaching from the starboard (right) side.

- If it is approaching from port (the left) then you are the 'stand on' vessel.

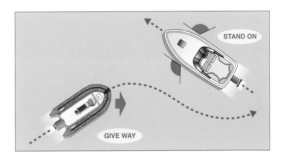

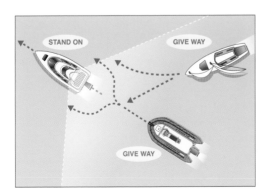

Overtaking

An overtaking vessel (one which falls within an arc of 135° at the rear of the craft being overtaken) must keep well clear of the vessel it is overtaking. The vessel being overtaken must maintain its course and speed.

Giving way to vessels under sail

- Powerboats unless being overtaken must give way to vessels under sail, passing astern.

- Keep well clear of sailing vessels as they may make large adjustments to their course as they 'tack' or 'gybe'. Remember, your wash can seriously disturb smaller craft.

- A yacht sailing with the assistance of its engine is 'motor sailing' and should display a cone with the point facing downwards in the rigging. The yacht is then classed as a motorised vessel under the rules.

Knowing under what circumstances sailing vessels give way to each other can help you decide what action to take when you are approaching them.

Sailing vessels cannot sail directly into wind and therefore use a zig zag course (tack) upwind.

Whether a sailing vessel is the give way vessel or the stand on vessel, is determined by which 'tack' it is on. The tack a yacht is on is indicated by looking at its sails, and by which side of the yacht the wind is blowing into. If the wind is blowing into the sails over the port side of the craft then it is on 'port tack'. If the wind is blowing over the starboard side into the sails it is 'starboard tack'.

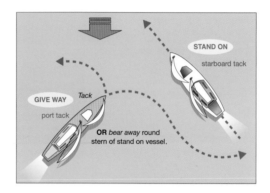

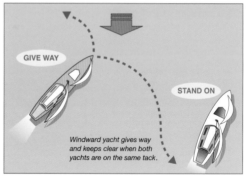

When both yachts are on the same track the yacht closest to the wind is called the 'windward' yacht and must keep clear.

Restricted visibility

When visibility is restricted, proceed at a safe, slow speed and use all available means to keep a lookout. Vessels fitted with radar should make best use of it. If possible head for shallower water away from larger vessels.

Lights, shapes and sounds

At night vessels display navigation lights to indicate the type of vessel and the position of the lights helps indicate the vessel's direction. By day, shapes are hoisted to indicate the nature of the vessel.

Fog signals
— One long blast (4-6 seconds)○ One short blast (2 seconds)

	At night	By Day
A vessel under 7m and 7 knots. A single white light could also be a vessel at anchor or a vessel seen from astern.		
A powered vessel under 50m shows a white masthead light, a white stern light and port and starboard lights. Fog — every two minutes.		
A powered craft over 50m displays two masthead white lights – the forward one lower than the one at the stern – a white stenlight and its port and starboard lights. Fog — every two minutes.		
A yacht under sail either shows a tricolour; or port and starboard lights plus a white sternlight. If the engine is used, it becomes a power vessel and must display the appropriate lights. Its day shape when motor sailing is a cone pointing downward. Fog — ○ ○ every two minutes.		
At anchor under 50m only one white light is required. The day shape is a black ball. A vessel over 50m at anchor displays two white lights, with the one at the stern lower than the one at the bow. <100m Fog rapid ringing of bell for 5 seconds every minute >100m Bell rung forward, gong aft for 5 seconds every minute.		
Code flag A indicates a vessel engaged in diving operations – keep well clear. At night restricted ability to manoeuvre lights are shown.		

	At night	By Day
A vessel 'not under command', (perhaps a vessel adrift with no means of propulsion) displays two all-round red lights at night or two balls in daylight. Fog — o o every two minutes.		
If constrained by draught the vessel displays 3 all round vertical red lights or a cylinder during the day. Fog — o o every two minutes.		
Vessels 'Restricted in ability to manoeuvre' show an additional all round red-white-red combination of lights at night and ball diamond ball in daylight. Fog — o o every two minutes.		
Vessel engaged in fishing (but not trawling), display an additional all-round red light above its all round white. Two cones apex together by day. Fog — o o every two minutes.		
A vessel trawling displays an additional all-round green light above its all round white. Two cones apex together by day. Fog — o o every two minutes.		
A vessel involved in dredging shows restricted in its ability to manoeuvre, plus two all-round vertical reds to show which side its gear is out and two all-round vertical greens showing the side that is safe to pass. In daylight, diamonds indicate the safe side and balls indicate the side not to pass.		
A vessel towing displays an additional white masthead light if the tow is less than 200m, or two additional white masthead lights, if it is greater than 200m. By day diamonds are shown. Fog — o o every two minutes. For both types.	OVER 200m / UNDER 200m	OVER 200m / UNDER 200m

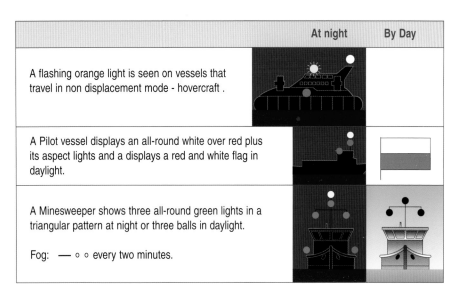

	At night	By Day
A flashing orange light is seen on vessels that travel in non displacement mode - hovercraft .		
A Pilot vessel displays an all-round white over red plus its aspect lights and a displays a red and white flag in daylight.		
A Minesweeper shows three all-round green lights in a triangular pattern at night or three balls in daylight. Fog: — ○ ○ every two minutes.		

Sounds can be used to indicate what a vessel is about to do. You should have the equipment to make them on board.

One short blast	"I am turning to starboard".
Two short blasts	"I am turning to port".
Three short blasts	"My engines are going astern" – this does not necessarily mean the craft is going backwards.
Five or more short blasts	"I don't understand your intentions" – perhaps better known as "What on earth are you doing?"

Traffic separation

Traffic separation schemes are denoted on a chart by purple shaded areas. Arrows on the chart denote the direction of the shipping lane. Traffic separation schemes separate large vessels in areas of heavy traffic. They keep all east bound vessels on one side and west bound on the other. Always keep your vessel at right angles to the scheme so that you show the correct aspect to oncoming traffic.

17 | Buoyage

Two buoyage systems exist in the world, IALA A and IALA B. The difference affects the colour and light characteristics of lateral marks.

IALA A is used in Europe, Russia, India, Australia and New Zealand.

IALA B is used in the USA, South America and parts of the Caribbean, South East Asia and Canada.

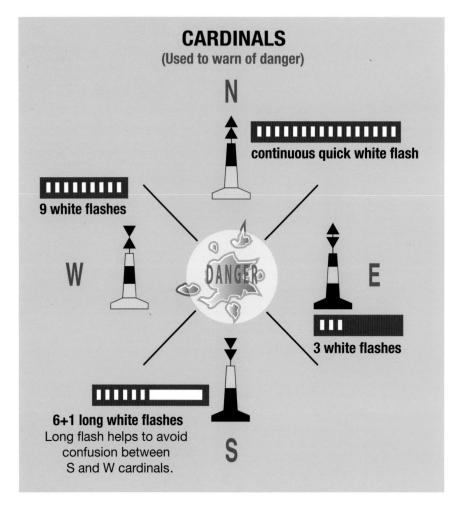

CARDINALS
(Used to warn of danger)

N — continuous quick white flash

9 white flashes — W

DANGER

E — 3 white flashes

6+1 long white flashes
Long flash helps to avoid confusion between S and W cardinals. — S

Cardinals

Cardinal marks warn of danger and remain constant throughout the IALA system. The cones always point to the black bands.

IALA - A Buoyage

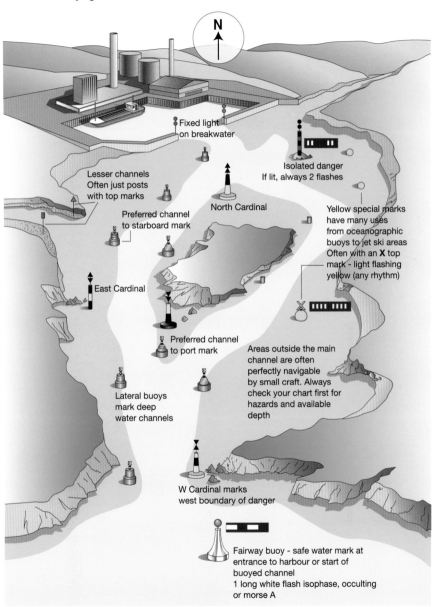

N

Fixed light on breakwater

Isolated danger
If lit, always 2 flashes

Lesser channels
Often just posts
with top marks

North Cardinal

Preferred channel
to starboard mark

Yellow special marks
have many uses
from oceanographic
buoys to jet ski areas
Often with an **X** top
mark - light flashing
yellow (any rhythm)

East Cardinal

Preferred channel
to port mark

Areas outside the main
channel are often
perfectly navigable
by small craft. Always
check your chart first for
hazards and available
depth

Lateral buoys
mark deep
water channels

W Cardinal marks
west boundary of danger

Fairway buoy - safe water mark at
entrance to harbour or start of
buoyed channel
1 long white flash isophase, occulting
or morse A

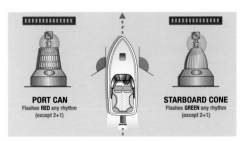

PORT CAN
Flashes RED any rhythm
(except 2+1)

STARBOARD CONE
Flashes GREEN any rhythm
(except 2+1)

Lateral marks

Used to mark channels.

In IALA A leave starboard cone to
your starboard side when going into
harbour.

IALA - B Buoyage

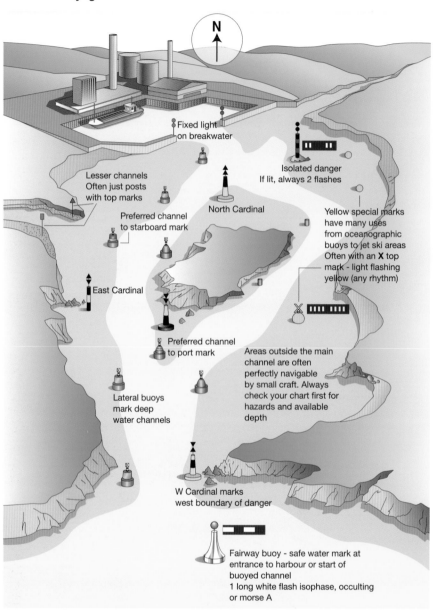

N

Fixed light
on breakwater

Lesser channels
Often just posts
with top marks

Preferred channel
to starboard mark

North Cardinal

East Cardinal

Isolated danger
If lit, always 2 flashes

Yellow special marks
have many uses
from oceanographic
buoys to jet ski areas
Often with an **X** top
mark - light flashing
yellow (any rhythm)

Preferred channel
to port mark

Lateral buoys
mark deep
water channels

Areas outside the main
channel are often
perfectly navigable
by small craft. Always
check your chart first for
hazards and available
depth

W Cardinal marks
west boundary of danger

Fairway buoy - safe water mark at
entrance to harbour or start of
buoyed channel
1 long white flash isophase, occulting
or morse A

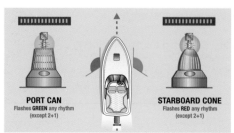

PORT CAN
Flashes **GREEN** any rhythm
(except 2+1)

STARBOARD CONE
Flashes **RED** any rhythm
(except 2+1)

Lateral marks

Used to mark channels.

In IALA B leave starboard cone to
your starboard side when going
into harbour.

Light sequences

Light Symbols on a chart refer to the way in which the light on a buoy flashes. The commonest types are:

NAME	CHART SYMBOL	DESCRIPTION	VISUALLY
Fixed	F	Fixed light - always on	
Flashing	Fl	Flashing, off more than on	
Group flashing	Fl (2)	Flashing in groups	
Long flashing	LFl	Flashing, off more than on but on lasting 2 or more seconds	
Quick	Q	50 - 79 flashes per min	
Very quick	VQ	80 - 90 flashes per min	
Group quick	Q (9)	A group of quick flashes followed by a period off	
Interrupted quick	IQ	Similar to group quick but with no specified number of flashes	
Isophase	Iso	Equally on and off	
Occulting	Oc	More on than off	
Alternating	Al.WR	Colour changes	
Fixed and flashing	F Fl(2)	Fixed light with flashes at higher intensity	

Sectored lights

At the entrance to harbours, sectored lights are sometimes found.

By staying in the white, or 'safe', area, a safe approach can be made at night.

In the red sector- too far to port

Safest approach is in the white sector

In the green sector- too far to starboard

18 Navigation

Charts

Charts are the nautical equivalent of road maps. They contain a wealth of valuable information and are an essential item for all craft.

When the world was first mapped, a method was needed to transfer what appeared on the spherical Earth to a flat sheet of paper. The method most commonly used is called Mercator's projection. This can be visualised as the image that would be cast on a sheet of paper wrapped around the globe, with a bright light at the centre.

To define a precise position on the Earth's surface two sets of lines are 'drawn' on the Earth. One set of lines runs North-South between the poles and are called meridians of longitude and the other set runs horizontally around the Earth and are called parallels of latitude.

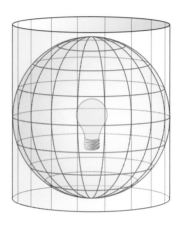

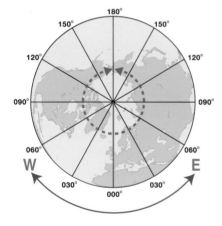

Looking down at the North Pole, the red line represents the 0° line of the Greenwich meridian. Positions are either East or West of the Greenwich Meridian 000°.

Looking from a different direction, the effect is segments of the earth. The lines can be defined for example, 030°W would put us somewhere on the 030° line.

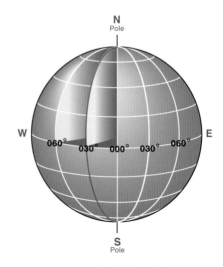

Latitude

The parallel lines of latitude 'slice' the Earth into layers; any one of these lines of latitude can be defined by its angle relative to the Equator.

Therefore precise positions on the Earth's surface can be referred to by a line of latitude and a line of longitude.

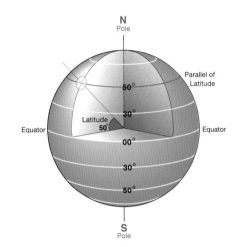

A basic position can be defined as such:

50° 00'.0 N, 030° 00'.O W

Each degree can be divided into fractions of a degree. Like hours, a degree consists of 60 minutes, and each minute consists of 60 seconds. Seconds are now usually expressed as decimals, so 42'30" becomes 42'.5

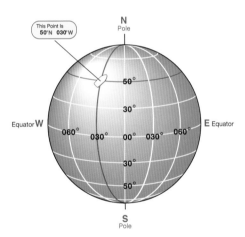

In the above example, the craft is 50 degrees north (50°N); one degree of latitude equals 60 nautical miles, therefore one minute of latitude equals one nautical mile (equals 1852m on land). So in this example, 50° x 60 miles = 3000 miles north of the Equator. If relaying this position verbally, you would say, "Five zero degrees north, zero three zero degrees west."

Rarely though does a craft sit perfectly on such a precise position. For example, a more typical position might be 53°42'.5N, 001°02'.5W.

A chart is only accurate on the day it is printed. Harbour authorities move, add or remove, buoys. Always check in the bottom left hand corner of the chart to see when it was last updated. Regular correction notices are published, and from these you should update your charts.

Correction notices are printed in many boating magazines and can now be downloaded from the chart manufacturer's website.

The compass

A compass allows you to:

- Steer on a particular heading.
- Take bearings of known objects and plot your position.
- Monitor the bearing to assess the risk of collision with other craft.

It is an essential item of safety and navigational kit. There are a variety of types of compass:

Traditional steering compass

- Should be mounted so that you can easily see it from the helm position.
- Ensure that the model you buy suits your boat.
- The compass consists of a card floating in liquid (to damp its movement) attached to a magnet.

Hand-bearing compass

- Used for taking bearings to other objects.
- Used to check relative bearings in collision situations.
- Can be used to check ship's compass

Fluxgate compass

- Electronic variant of the traditional compass.
- Able to pass steering information to other devices such as autopilots.
- Carefully follow the instructions to avoid creating errors during use.

Gyro Compass

- Usually the preserve of large ships and is highly accurate and stable.
- Cheaper Gyro rate compasses being used by small boats to great affect.
- Can be interfaced with Autopilots.

In this example the powerboat's heading is 045°, the bearing of the craft to starboard is 080° and the rock to port is 340°.

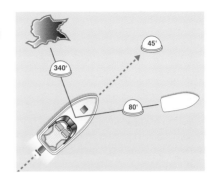

Variation

A compass points to Magnetic North rather than to the North Pole. On a chart, the vertical lines point to 'True' North.

This difference between True and Magnetic North is called variation. When transferring bearings from a chart to use on a compass, they need to be converted from True to Magnetic. Likewise, when reading bearings from a compass they need converting before plotting on a chart.

The Amount

True to magnetic: Add variation if west, subtract if east

For example:

True (T) = 107°, Variation (V) = 4°W

Magnetic = 107°T + 4°W = 111°M

Magnetic to true: Subtract variation if west, add if east

True = 111°M − 4°W = 107°T

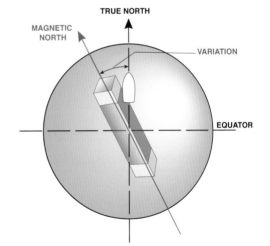

In the above example, if the Magnetic heading was 111°M, using the deviation table from page 88 the compass heading (C) will be 115°C (C = M (111°) + Westerly variation (4°).

Variation can vary greatly between different boating areas, and changes over time. It is calculated and recorded on charts.

Deviation

Deviation is the error caused by metal items (or electronic fields) on board affecting the compass reading. The error varies as the heading changes. To properly allow for deviation, a deviation card detailing the error at each heading is required.

The simplest way to create a deviation card is to compare the reading from the steering compass with the reading from a hand-bearing compass, which is held well clear of any possible interference. Do this for various headings, and then plot the errors to create your own deviation card. Alternatively a compass adjuster can swing the compass and create a card for you.

To adjust from Magnetic to Compass
(i.e. to adjust for deviation)

C = M + Westerly deviation

C = M – Easterly deviation

To adjust Compass to Magnetic

M = C – Westerly deviation

M = C + Easterly deviation

Tip - Remembering all these adjustments is not easy. In your boating area variation will probably always be either W or E, so just remember one of the equations, e.g., 'M = T + West Variation'. Deviation is then applied to the result and is vessel specific.

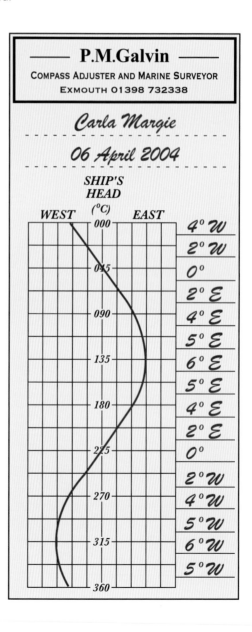

Tides and tidal streams

The gravitational effect of the Moon and Sun on the Earth are the main cause of tides.

Spring tides When the Earth is in line with the Moon and Sun, high tides are at their highest, and low tides at their lowest.

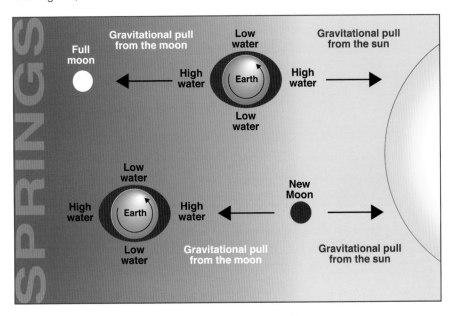

Neap tides: highs and lows are smaller than at spring tides.

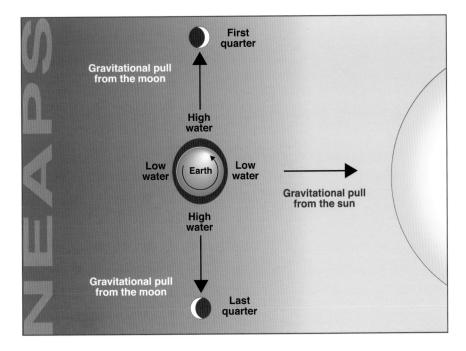

Knowing the tidal height allows the depth of water at a given position to be predicted by adding the tidal height to the charted depth.

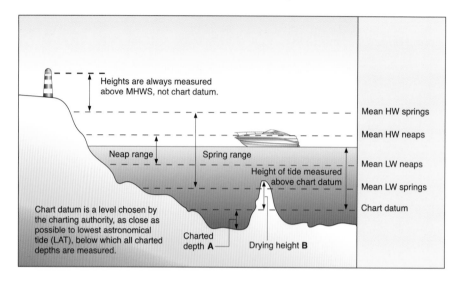

Heights are always measured above MHWS, not chart datum.

Mean HW springs

Mean HW neaps

Neap range

Spring range

Mean LW neaps

Height of tide measured above chart datum

Mean LW springs

Chart datum is a level chosen by the charting authority, as close as possible to lowest astronomical tide (LAT), below which all charted depths are measured.

Chart datum

Charted depth **A**

Drying height **B**

'A' is a charted depth. For example if this charted depth was 2.4m and you know the height of tide will be 0.8m, then the depth at that point is 2.4m + 0.8m = 3.2m.
'B' is a drying height: imagine it is 0.3m above chart datum in this example. The height of tide is 0.8m – 0.3m = 0.5m.

In most places high tides follow low tides on a roughly six hour cycle (i.e., two highs and two lows per day). Springs and neaps alternate on a seven day cycle.

Tidal information is available from a variety of sources:

- Nautical almanacs contain a wealth of information. Tidal data is shown in a table with the times of high water, low water, and the tidal height. Use this with the tidal curve for any location to calculate tidal heights at any time.

- Local tide tables/curves: Increasingly popular are the tidal curve booklets available for local areas. These are easy to use (see page 92).

- The Internet.

Tip - It's very easy to pick the wrong day or forget the correction for summertime so when you have gathered your tidal information always double check. Is the level of tide that you see on arrival at your launch site or marina the same as the almanac?

Tidal streams

Knowing the rate and direction of flow at a given time is important because:

- You can make your passage with the stream rather than push against it to give a faster passage.

- You can time your passage to avoid a dangerous situation, such as where wind is opposing stream making rougher water.

Tidal stream data is available in two forms:

Tidal stream atlas

Tidal stream maps are found in almanacs and tidal stream atlases. These show the direction and rate of the tide at hour intervals before and after high water. The figures '12,27' means that the rate at neaps is 1.2 knots, while at springs (which is always greater) it is 2.7 knots. The direction of the arrow gives the direction of flow.

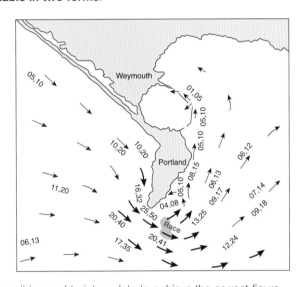

If between springs and neaps, it is usual to interpolate to achieve the correct figure.

Tidal diamonds

Tidal diamonds are found on charts. The figures which relate to these diamonds are found elsewhere on the chart and show the rate and direction of the tide at springs and neaps.

5606·3 — Tidal Streams referred to HW at DOVER

Hours	◇ Geographical Position	◇ 51°16'3N 1 27·3E	◇ 51°09'0N 1 27·7E	◇ 51°06'6N 1 33·2E	◇ 51°15'2N 1 33·4E	◇ 51°20·3N 1 34·2E	◇ 51°13·0N 1 36·0E	◇ 51°09'5N 1 44·0E	◇ 51°13'0N 1 52·9E	
Before High Water	6	195 20 11	212 22 12	219 11 06	226 25 14	199 20 12	190 09 05	231 22 12	225 09 06	-6
	5	197 26 15	213 22 12	227 25 14	230 31 17	204 26 15	191 23 13	218 22 12	224 16 08	-5
	4	197 28 15	216 19 11	225 36 20	231 34 19	208 31 17	195 31 17	213 28 16	219 19 09	-4
	3	202 24 13	228 13 08	224 32 18	234 33 18	213 28 15	196 32 18	206 26 15	215 17 07	-3
	2	215 10 06	00 00	220 18 10	233 16 09	222 15 08	195 20 11	207 15 08	207 13 04	-2
	1	012 13 07	032 12 07	050 04 02	049 08 04	357 08 05	00 00	053 04 02	174 06 02	-1
High Water		017 27 15	038 20 12	043 21 12	049 30 17	015 25 14	013 13 07	040 18 10	048 12 07	0
After High Water	1	027 32 17	039 23 13	046 30 16	046 37 21	023 32 18	015 24 14	035 23 13	045 16 09	+1
	2	018 26 14	034 22 12	044 32 18	049 34 19	029 29 16	014 31 17	040 23 13	042 19 09	+2
	3	022 17 09	031 15 08	040 24 13	057 24 13	044 22 13	017 26 15	030 19 10	036 18 08	+3
	4	037 06 03	00 00	038 09 06	065 09 05	059 12 07	018 17 10	023 12 07	028 10 04	+4
	5	206 04 02	203 10 06	00 00	224 05 03	00 00	018 06 03	345 04 02	025 04 01	+5
	6	197 16 09	210 18 10	210 08 04	225 21 12	197 14 08	189 05 03	246 07 04	235 06 03	+6

Tip - When the direction of a tide is quoted (e.g. 090°) this is the direction the tide flows towards.

Tidal curves

If you want to know the tidal height between the times of high and low water you can use a tidal curve to calculate the tidal height at any time.

A tidal curve shows how the tide varies between high and low water. They are found in almanacs for major boating locations.

To use a tidal curve:

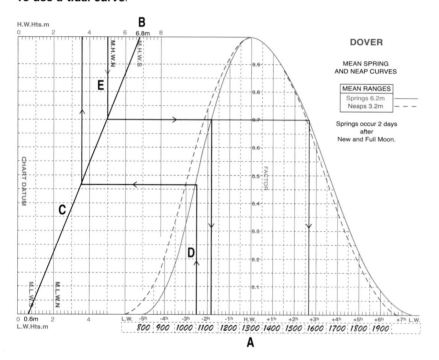

- Find the tidal data from the almanac for the day concerned. The almanac will tell you which 'Standard port' and curve to use for your location – in this case Dover.

- Adjust high water time to Daylight Saving Time (if required) and enter it in box (A). In this example HW is at 1300 DST.

- Fill in the remaining boxes in one hour increments either side of HW.

- Mark the HW and LW tidal heights onto the graph (B) and connect them with a line (C).

- Calculate the 'tidal range' (difference in height between HW and LW), by subtracting the LW height from the HW height. A small box on the curve indicates which curve line to use. In this example 6.8m – 0.6m = 6.2m range. 6.2 range = springs, therefore the solid curve line (red) is used.

You can now use the curve to calculate the tidal heights from the curve.

Example:

- To find the tidal height at 10.30am, draw a vertical line (Line D) from the 10.30 time until it intersects the curve. Then run the line to the diagonal depth line and up to read off the height. It reads as 3.6m.

- To find when the tidal height will be 5.0m. Draw a vertical line from the tidal height scale (E) down to the diagonal line, then across to the curve.

- The two points either side, where it bisects the curve, will give you the times when the height is 5.0m. At any time between these times the tide is in excess of this height. The times read as between about 1110 and 1540.

Rule of Twelfths

If you want to know the tidal height at a given time but do not have a tidal curve to hand, you can approximate roughly using the rule of twelfths. The rule assumes that the rise and fall of tide is symmetrical and occurs every six hours.

This rule suggests:

- 1st hour – 1/12th of tide rises or falls
- 2nd hour – 2/12ths of tide rises or falls
- 3rd hour – 3/12ths of tide rises or falls
- 4th hour – 3/12ths of tide rises or falls
- 5th hour – 2/12ths of tide rises or falls
- 6th hour – 1/12th of tide rises or falls

For example:

HW = 4.8m at 0600.

LW = 1.2m at 1200.

What is the tidal height at 1100?

- The range is 3.6m (4.8m – 1.2m).
- 1100 is 1 hour before low water.
- The fall of the tide in the last hour is 1/12th x 3.6m = 0.3m.
- So 1 hour before low water the tidal height will be 0.3m + 1.2m = 1.5m.

What the rule of twelfths also graphically illustrates is that far more tide flows in the 3rd and 4th hours than at other times, therefore the tidal rate is also greater.

However, the rule of twelfths doesn't apply in every location.

Tip - Remember the tidal height is not the depth of water. Add it to the figures on the chart to calculate the depth at that point.

Tip - Some areas have unusual tidal characteristics and the tidal curves may be drawn around low water.

Chart basics

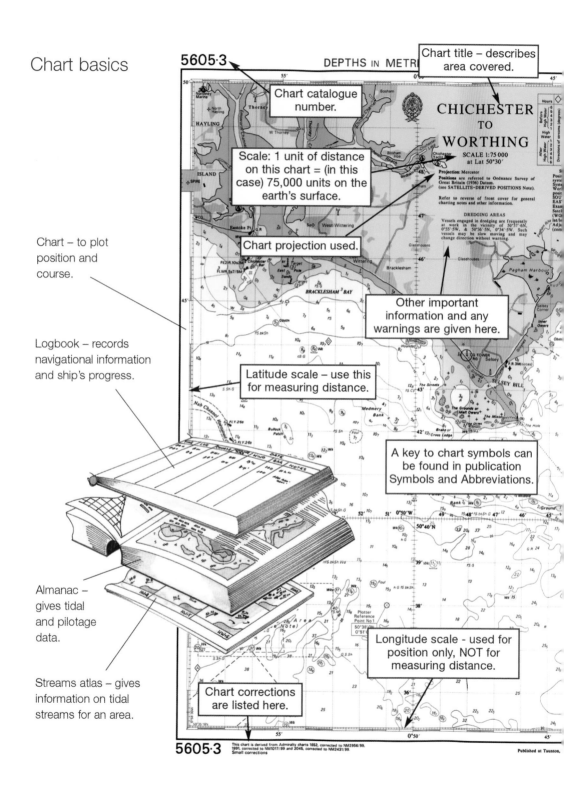

Chart title – describes area covered.

Chart catalogue number.

Scale: 1 unit of distance on this chart = (in this case) 75,000 units on the earth's surface.

Chart projection used.

Chart – to plot position and course.

Other important information and any warnings are given here.

Logbook – records navigational information and ship's progress.

Latitude scale – use this for measuring distance.

A key to chart symbols can be found in publication Symbols and Abbreviations.

Almanac – gives tidal and pilotage data.

Longitude scale - used for position only, NOT for measuring distance.

Streams atlas – gives information on tidal streams for an area.

Chart corrections are listed here.

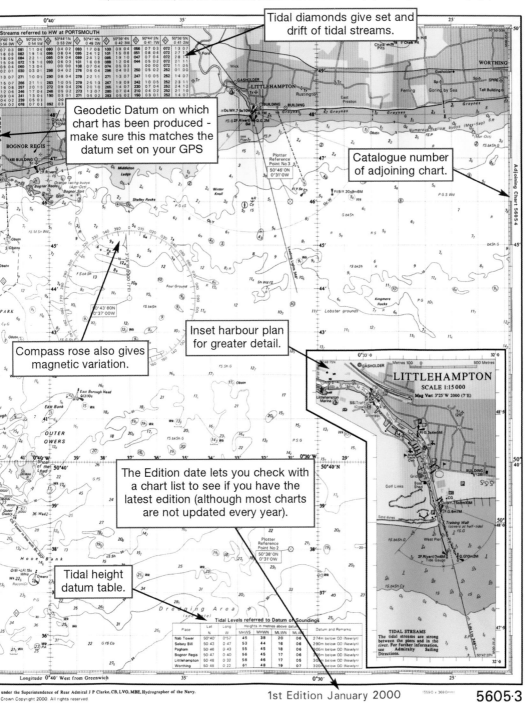

Tidal diamonds give set and drift of tidal streams.

Geodetic Datum on which chart has been produced - make sure this matches the datum set on your GPS

Catalogue number of adjoining chart.

Compass rose also gives magnetic variation.

Inset harbour plan for greater detail.

The Edition date lets you check with a chart list to see if you have the latest edition (although most charts are not updated every year).

Tidal height datum table.

1st Edition January 2000

5605·3

Passage making

By bringing together an understanding of charts, tides, compasses plus latitude and longitude we can plan routes and passages and move safely between two points.

Position fixing

A fix is generally taken from a GPS, however it is essential to understand how to manually plot one as well.

Bearings are taken with a hand bearing compass although one fitted to the boat can be used.

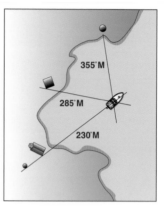

3 Point Fix

- Look for easily identifiable positions on the chart and ashore.

- Ensure they are 50-100° apart to achieve a good cut.

- Note down the bearings and the time and log reading.

- Convert the bearings to 'true' and plot them.

- Where they cross is your position - mark time and log on the chart.

- Double check this by other means – depth or a good look around.

- A Cocked Hat is where you have a triangle of intersection.

- The position is historical and refers to a particular time and log reading.

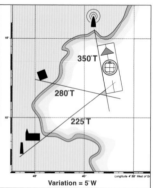

Variation = 5'W

Chartwork

Chartwork allows us to work out our intended passage or where we should be from where we have been. We use plotting symbols on the chart to make it easy to follow.

Symbol	Description	Symbol	Description
⊙	Fix		Fix obtained by ranges
⊿	Estimated position		
⊢——⊣	Dead reckoning position	——→	Water track
⊕	Waypoint (WPT)	——≫	Ground track
	Fix from visual bearings	——⋙	Tidal set and drift

Measuring distance on a chart

When measuring distance, always take the dividers to the 'latitude' scale on the side of the chart alongside the area that you are measuring.

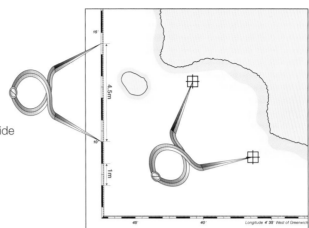

Plotting a Position

To plot a position on a chart from a latitude and longitude:

- Mark off the latitude by marking a line from the vertical scale in the area you expect it to intersect the meridian of longitude.

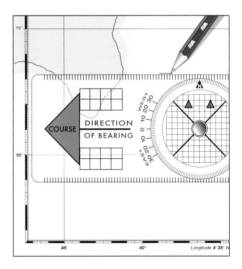

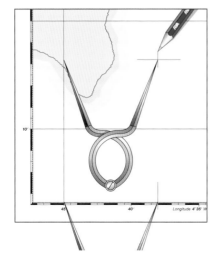

- Mark off the meridian of longitude from the horizontal scale at the top or bottom of the chart.

- Where the lines intersect is the position.

Tip - When plotting you can either use a plotter or dividers. A plotter is easier on a small powerboat.

Using depth contours for a fix

Depth contours can be used both as an aid to fixing a position and to navigate by following along them.

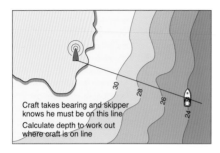

Craft takes bearing and skipper knows he must be on this line

Calculate depth to work out where craft is on line

Take a bearing and check the depth. The position must be close to this depth contour line.

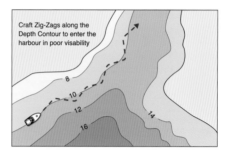

Craft Zig-Zags along the Depth Contour to enter the harbour in poor visability

The actual depth will be the charted depths from the chart plus rise of tide.

Estimating your position (EP)

The same principles can be used to estimate where you are or where you will end up. The terms used are 'dead reckoning' (DR) and 'estimated position' (EP).

For example, a craft achieves 15 knots on a heading of 080°T. Plot the line on a chart depicting the water track. The point on the line that the craft has reached after a certain period of time is its position – this is dead reckoning. It may not be very accurate as it ignores stream. Add in the tidal vector for the same time period for a far more accurate estimate – your estimated position. This can be repeated for different speeds, headings and tidal streams to represent your journey.

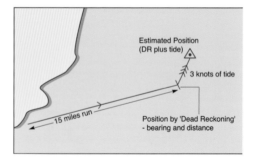

Estimated Position (DR plus tide)

3 knots of tide

15 miles run

Position by 'Dead Reckoning' - bearing and distance

Leeway

Leeway is the effect the wind has on a craft. At speed, powerboats are affected far less by the wind than yachts or slower motorboats. High sided craft in windy conditions may need to adjust for leeway. If wind is blowing on your beam, assume that you need to adjust by 5° or 10° by altering your heading to steer more into the wind. If the wind increases you may need to allow for more leeway.

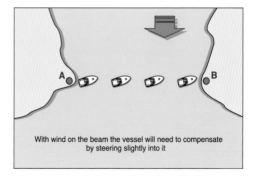

A   B

With wind on the beam the vessel will need to compensate by steering slightly into it

Course to Steer

In some areas a simple course can be laid on the chart and that course steered. In areas where there is stream things are different. If the boat heads directly at the target point, the stream may push it off the track. In this case a compensation for this effect is made by altering the heading.

To calculate to allow for a cross stream and find what the revised heading should be:

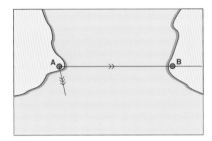

- Draw a line from A through B and beyond.
- This is the Ground Track (two arrows denotes Ground Track).
- From A plot the 'Tidal Vector' (three arrows). In this case the Tidal Rate is 170°T 1.3 knots so plot 1.3M.

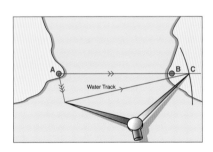

- Open the compass to the distance the craft would travel in 1 hour.
- This craft at 5 knots would travel 5 miles in 1 hour.
- Mark off where the compass intersects the line A-B making point C.
- Join these two points, this is the water track (1 arrow).

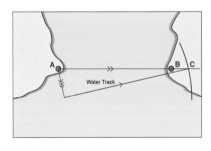

- Read the angle of the water track.
- This is the 'Course to Steer'.
- This will need adjusting from True to Magnetic.
- The distance A-C is the actual distance the craft will travel in 1 hour.
- This is the 'Speed Over Ground'.

In this example the size of the vector diagram fits comfortably onto the chart. The diagram can be plotted over a 30 minute period rather than an hour, as shown, if that fits better, e.g., plot a half hour ground track, a half hour tidal vector, and so on.

Tip - If you are undertaking a long passage, the rate and direction of the tide will vary often. In this case you can undertake a series of these calculations for each hour of the journey – do not assume that the tide direction and rate will remain constant during the passage.

Electronic navigation

GPS for navigation

The GPS (Global Positioning System) has become the centrepiece of most boaters' navigation 'toolbox'. It is best used in addition to, rather than instead of, more traditional navigation methods.

GPS receivers calculate their position by reference to a number of satellites that orbit the Earth. Receivers come in many shapes, from hand-held units to sets built-in to the boat. They are typically accurate to between 10m and 15m and the positions are displayed in latitude and longitude. Because a GPS knows where you are and where you were, they also deduce the boat's speed and course over ground.

Waypoints

A waypoint is a predetermined point along the intended track and is entered into the set as a latitude and longitude. The GPS will calculate the distance and bearing from its current position to give a course. Once the vessel starts to move to the waypoint, it will also calculate the estimated time of arrival at the waypoint and whether the boat is straying either side of the direct course line.

Waypoints and GPS sets are not intelligent, just computers. They will always take the shortest route from A-B even though this may be over land or rocks. Therefore several waypoints are used to form a route to keep the boat away from danger.

Using your GPS

- Waypoint entry - ensure that the latitude and longitude is double checked.

- Ensure the waypoints or course does not cross over dangers.

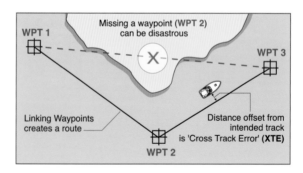

- Plot your intended route on a chart and double check the bearing and distance compared to the GPS.

- Link waypoints together to form a route.

- Ensure that the GPS receiver is set to the same datum as the chart. GPS positions default to WGS 84 datum as used on newer charts.

- A GPS set can be setup to display positions in the same format as the chart.

- Keep a log of your position, so that in the event of system failure you can continue your route.

Goto a waypoint

A GPS usually has a few different screens that can be used to steer to a waypoint. The usual screens are a rolling road or a compass needle that points in the required direction.

Cross Track Error XTE and Waypoint Ladder

The problem with straying off the intended track is that dangers may lurk either side of the direct line. Straying either side of the line is called 'cross track error' (XTE) and an alarm can be set on the GPS after deciding an acceptable XTE for your route.

This is usually just shown on a GPS screen. Visually on a chart it would look like a waypoint ladder.

To create a waypoint ladder simply draw a line between two waypoints and mark off lines at 0.5 or 1m intervals to form a ladder. When running between the waypoints you can read off distance and XTE and easily plot your position alongside the 'ladder' or gauge your position by eye.

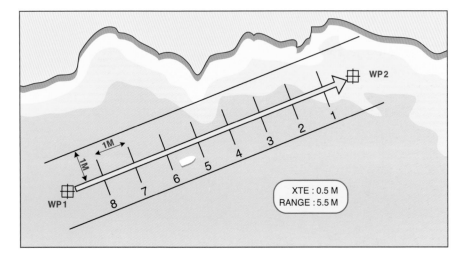

GPS techniques

Laboriously plotting latitude and longitude at speed is time consuming and difficult on a powerboat, therefore other techniques can be used to get the best out of a GPS in conjunction with a paper chart. The quickest way to get a position is by using bearing and distance to a waypoint.

Waypoint web

Plot a waypoint on the chart (C). From the waypoint, draw a series of lines at different bearings and use a compass to draw arcs of distance from the waypoint. Then as you head towards the waypoint, it is easy to read off the distance and bearing of the waypoint and to plot your position on the 'web'. This technique is very useful at night or in rough conditions.

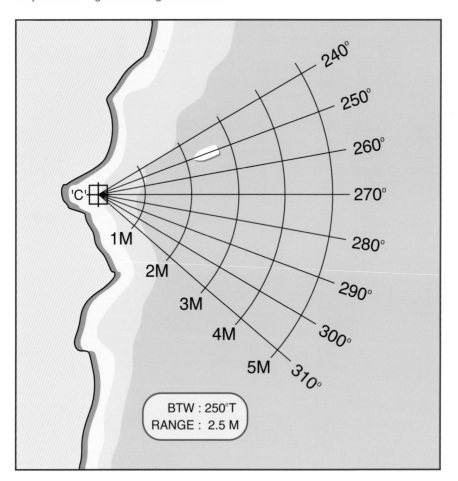

Compass rose waypoint

An adaption of this is to use a compass rose on a waypoint. Enter a waypoint from the centre of a compass rose on the chart. Select 'goto' that waypoint. The GPS will tell you the bearing and distance to that waypoint. You can now plot your position easily and accurately onto the chart. Check to see that the GPS is configured to give the bearing in 'True'.

Chart plotters

Chart plotters combine a GPS set with a series of electronic charts depicted on a colour or black and white screen, so that the boat's position is graphically displayed. Waypoints and routes are added by moving a cursor onto the desired point instead of entering lat and long numbers. Typically, charts are held on a small data card inserted into the machine.

Advantages:

- The boat is graphically displayed on a chart for instant position information.
- Waypoints and routes are easy to plot and check for accuracy. The safety of your route can be assessed quickly.
- The chart can be zoomed in and extra detail added or removed according to need.
- A small data card can hold a considerable number of charts.

Disadvantages:

- Electronics can fail – electronic charts should be backed up with paper charts.
- Screen size is important as it allows the 'bigger picture' to be viewed. Large screens are expensive.

Radar

Radar works by sending out radio waves that rebound off a solid object, back to the radar. These radio echoes are then displayed on a screen. The size and strength of the echo depends on what is reflected. A tanker will give a better echo than a small wooden sailing boat.

To increase a small boats echo, radar reflectors are placed on the flybridge or deck head to amplify the signal return. Even if radar is fitted, a reflector is still required.

Radar is now fitted into a growing number of smaller boats. Radar and chart plotter systems can be integrated to display on the same screen. The images can be overlaid or viewed as separate screens. They are excellent for use at night and in restricted visibility. However, bear in mind:

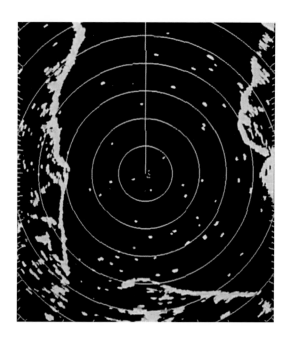

- Radar is not as intuitive as a chart plotter or GPS. Taking a training course to understand their use is a good idea.

- The ability to interpret what you see grows with experience. Practise in good conditions before you use the system for real.

- Radar can display the picture in 'North-up', 'Course-up', or 'Head-up' mode. Make sure that you know what you are looking at.

- This radar screen and chart are depicting the same area. The radar is in 'Course-up', the chart is in 'North-up'.

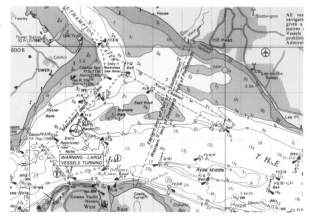

Passage planning and pilotage

Passage planning; is the preparation of a plan that helps you safely navigate between two areas.

Pilotage; is what you do at either end of your passage and is the use of buoyage, depth and transits, to safely manoeuvre your craft into or out of a harbour or marina.

Where you are going will define what will be in your plan and how you 'record' it. A skipper undertaking a passage needs to consider a variety of factors:

Weather

- What is it doing now and how will it change over the duration of the passage?
- How will it affect your passage (e.g. wind against stream).
- Can you update weather information during the journey?

The route

- Have charts of a suitable scale for the route and harbours that will, or may be, entered.
- Create the route and document headings, waypoints, distances, times, speeds, depths etc.
- Record dangerous, key or useful features on route.

Tidal heights and streams

- Is there enough water to enter and exit the harbour and undertake the passage?
- When should the passage commence to avoid unfavourable conditions (e.g., wind against stream) and to ensure safe entry to the destination port?

Pilotage

- Plan harbour entry or exits, note important features such as marks and lights.
- Repeat for ports of refuge.

There is no right way to record a passage plan, and a skipper must make a judgement call as to what approach best suits the passage being made. A short trip to a local bay is technically a passage but does not necessarily require a written plan if thought has gone into the passage. A 15 mile trip along the coast, though, would benefit from a fairly detailed (but simple) document addressing all of the above.

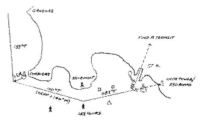

Simple pilotage plan

Tip - A sensible skipper ensures that someone (be it the Coastguard or a friend) knows where he intends going and when he should be there.

19 | Weather

Weather plays a fundamental role in your decision whether to go to sea. Being able to assess the weather conditions you may encounter during the intended passage is a basic requirement of a skipper. With experience you are able to read a weather forecast and make a judgement based on it.

Causes of weather

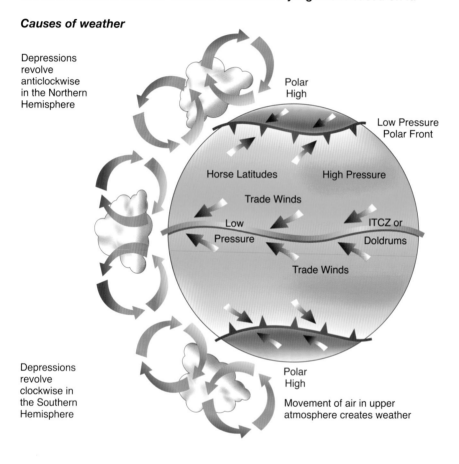

Depressions revolve anticlockwise in the Northern Hemisphere

Polar High

Low Pressure Polar Front

Horse Latitudes

High Pressure

Trade Winds

Low Pressure

ITCZ or Doldrums

Trade Winds

Depressions revolve clockwise in the Southern Hemisphere

Polar High

Movement of air in upper atmosphere creates weather

The weather systems that we experience are caused by the movement of air created by the warming of the Earth. Hot air at the Equator rises and is replaced by cooler air moving in from elsewhere. The irregular distribution of land and water masses create a pattern of hot and cold areas producing bands of high and low pressure like corridors around the Earth. Spinning of the Earth allows these highs and lows to move, collide and mix with each other causing weather systems.

Weather map

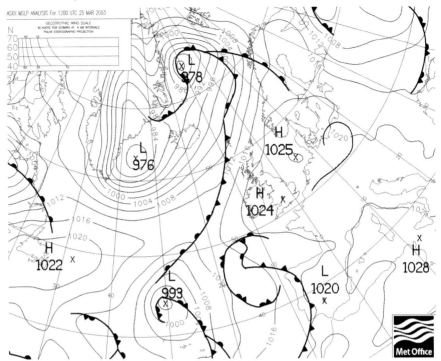

Isobars

The lines on a weather chart linking areas of equal pressure are called isobars. The closer these lines are together, the greater the pressure gradient and the greater the wind speed. Steady barometric pressure usually means steady wind, whereas pressure changing rapidly means a stronger wind.

High pressure areas, or 'anticyclones', typically give good, settled weather with light winds and clear skies. On weather maps a high pressure system will typically have widely spaced isobars indicating less strong winds. Winds travel clockwise around the anticyclone in the Northern Hemisphere and anticlockwise in the Southern Hemisphere.

In contrast, depressions are areas of low pressure usually with stronger winds. They revolve anticlockwise in the Northern Hemisphere and the opposite in the Southern Hemisphere. Depressions arise where the colder air meets warmer air making a warm and cold front. Cold fronts move more rapidly than warm fronts and therefore catch them up. A merged warm and cold front turns into an 'occluded' front.

Depressions are typified by:

- unsettled weather.
- rainfall – often heavy.
- strong winds.
- a general direction of travel from west to east.

Types of cloud in a depression

Cumulus	Low cloud and rain	Altostratus thickening to nimbostratus	Cirrostratus	High cirrus cloud
As the cold front arrives, the pressure can drop again. There may be heavy rain, strong winds and perhaps thunderstorms. The cloud is cumulus or cumulonimbus.	In the warm sector, the barometer stops falling. The rain either ceases or eases but the cloud base is low with poor visibility.	The cloud continues to thicken becoming nimbostratus and the cloud level has lowered. As the front approaches it begins to rain.	The cloud has thickened into cirrostratus and the barometer continues to fall. The wind direction 'backs' (moves anticlockwise) often from a SW direction to southerly.	The high, thin cirrus clouds indicate the approach of a depression (12–24 hours away). The barometer starts to fall.

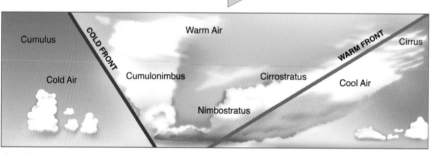

Sunshine and showers

Heaviest rain just ahead of the cold front. Grey drizzly conditions

As the warm front approaches cloud lowers and thickens until it rains

A barograph trace - there is likely to be a definite kick as the cold front passes

Barometer readings as fronts pass

The depression is passing from west to east; the warm front appears first, followed by the cold front. In some areas, especially in the Southern Hemisphere, the warm front is hardly noticed but the cold front brings worsening weather.

Tip - The way pressure is rising or falling can tell you much about the likely weather to follow. Rapidly falling or rising pressure indicates very unsettled weather ahead. A rise or fall of 4mb within three hours usually indicates strong winds, and a change of 6mb indicates a possible gale.

Sea breezes

Sea breezes are caused by the flow of air from the sea to the land to fill the void created by the rising of hot air as it is warmed over land. Sea breezes occur in the afternoon on clear, hot sunny days. They always blow onshore and their strength can be increased or decreased by the actual wind direction.

Early stages of sea breeze developing. Heat rising over the land is creating the line of clouds

Fog

Being caught in fog can be a very frightening and dangerous experience for a boater. The most common types of fog are caused by the cooling of the air to a point where moisture in the air condenses into droplets.

The three main types of fog are:

- **Radiation fog** - this tends to occur overnight and disperses rapidly as the ground warms. Caused by the rapidly cooling land where a warm, moist airstream exists.

- **Advection fog** - caused by the passage of warm moist air over the cold water. Requires a drier airstream to clear it – also known as 'Sea fog'.

- **Frontal fog** - may occur at a warm front, and tends not to persist. Caused by warm air rising over cold air.

Sourcing weather forecasts

There are a variety of sources of weather forecasts and weather data that you can use:

The Internet	An increasingly popular source of forecasts with a wealth of data. Some weather files can even be downloaded and overlaid onto to a Navigation computer screen.
National and local radio	Many countries give a national shipping forecast that gives reasonable information but many tend to be too generalised and lack specific local information. Local radio stations near boating areas often broadcast excellent local forecasts.
VHF	Coastguard stations usually broadcast regular weather forecasts on the VHF radio. These forecasts often cover very specific areas and are extremely useful. Some areas of the world use VHF weather channels that continuously broadcast the current forecast.
Commercial services	Commercial forecasting services offer a phone/fax/sms service with both the National forecast and local forecasts.
Marinas and harbour masters	Can generally be relied upon to post copies of the inshore waters forecast alongside a weather chart for the day.
Newspapers and television	Local TV stations often broadcast reasonable data. However, forecasts on the national news are usually too general. Local newspapers can be useful but may lack detail.
Navtex	A radio receiver mainly fitted to larger craft, but also found in marinas, prints or displays weather forecasts and general safety broadcasts.

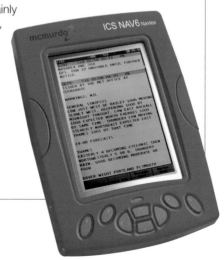

The Beaufort Scale and interpreting weather forecasts

Force	Wind speed	Description	Wave height	Sea state
0	< 1 knot	Calm	0m	Mirror like
1	1–3 knots	Light air	Up to 0.1m	Ripples on the surface
2	4–6 knots	Light breeze	Up to 0.3m	Small wavelets with smooth crests
3	7–10 knots	Gentle breeze	Up to 0.9m	Large wavelets with crests starting to break
4	11–16 knots	Moderate breeze	Up to 1.5m	Large waves begin to form with white foam crests
5	17–21 knots	Fresh breeze	Up to 2.5m	Moderate waves and many white horses
6	22–27 knots	Strong breeze	Up to 4m	Large waves, spray and white foam crests
7	28–33 knots	Near gale	Up to 5.5m	Breaking waves, a heaped sea, lots of spray
8	34–40 knots	Gale	Up to 7.5m	Frequently breaking, moderately high waves
9	41–47 knots	Severe gale	Up to 10m	High waves, flying spray and breaking crests
10	48–55 knots	Storm	Up to 12.5m	Very high waves, almost totally white, with foam and spray
11	56–63 knots	Violent storm	Up to 16m	Extensive foam, exceptionally high waves, visibility seriously affected
12	> 64 knots	Hurricane	16m +	Air filled with foam and spray, very poor visibility

Tip - A fairly easy to handle Force 4 for one craft may be the equivalent of storm force to another. Beware of and understand your vessel's limitations and that of its crew.

Developing the skills needed to interpret forecasts and predict weather takes time. One of the best ways to develop your capability is to listen to and read forecasts. Develop an understanding of different weather systems and continually compare what you see and experience with the forecasts.

20 | Boating at Night and in Restricted Visibility

What is a quite straightforward area to cruise during the day takes on a very different outlook after dark. Boating at night is usually planned but sometimes becomes necessary because of a delayed schedule or some other problem. Good preparation is the key.

Planning

- Create a plan for your trip and the detail of the harbour entrance. Ensure it is simple and clear so it can be easily interpreted in the dark.

- Note down the light characteristics of the buoys.

- Mark the dangers and hazards – unlit buoys and rocks.

- Follow a pre-planned course from buoy to buoy or waypoints to avoid dangers.

- Prepare the boat and crew. Dim the instrument and equipment lights to preserve night vision. Use red lights where possible.

- Wear lifejackets and ensure that they have lights fitted.

- Maintain a good lookout and be especially aware of pot markers and unlit buoys.

- If on a passage, plan a watch system.

Restricted visibility

Boating in fog can be one of the most dangerous situations for a small craft.

If fog is predicted, going to sea is foolhardy and should be avoided. If you are already at sea when fog descends, the safe option is to turn back and return to port or, if that is not a safe option, make way to a safe area away from shipping. Either way, as skipper your first responsibility is for your crew, and your actions should reflect this.

If you are already at sea

- Reduce speed to just a few knots.
- Confirm your position.
- All crew should wear lifejackets.
- Hoist a radar reflector.
- Switch on navigation lights.
- Sound the appropriate sound signal – usually 1 long blast every two minutes.
- Post a crew member to listen and look for other craft.
- Consider switching off the engine every few minutes to hear other craft.
- Confirm your position.
- If you are in a shipping lane or main channel, move to shallow water.
- Consider anchoring in shallow water until the fog lifts.

Whether or not you make a 'run for home' will be influenced by a variety of factors: where you are; your navigation skills; whether you possess a radar or chart plotter and the knowledge to competently use them; and how easy is the entry into the harbour. If you do decide to enter a harbour or marina, create a plan containing the information you will need to make a safe entry.

Tip - It is good practice to pre-enter your GPS with waypoints and routes into harbours you will pass by to act as 'ports of refuge' in the event of a problem.

21 | Trailing Your Boat

Trailing a boat can be a stressful, tiring experience or relatively straightforward – the difference is preparation.

Secure all equipment before trailing

Key points to remember are:

- Ensure your tow vehicle is up to the job. The combined weight of the trailer and boat should not exceed the permissible towing limit for the vehicle.

- Ensure the vehicle is capable of pulling the trailer up the slipways you intend using?

- In most situations if the combined weight of boat and trailer exceeds 750kg, the trailer needs to be fitted with brakes.

- Regularly grease and oil the trailer as necessary. Ensure wheel bearings are regularly repacked with fresh grease to enhance their life.

- Ensure that the trailer is set up for the boat it is to carry. See that rollers are well positioned and the transom of the boat, which carries the weight of the engine through to the trailer, is supported and does not overhang the rollers by more than about 50cm.

- When towing, tie the boat down to the trailer tightly. Any movement between the two can cause a lot of damage.

- Never immerse a trailer with hot wheel bearings into cold water, or the bearings will lose their grease and fail. Allow the bearings to cool for 45 minutes after a trip.

- Fit a safety chain between the trailer and the tow vehicle so that if the trailer breaks away it will stay with the tow vehicle.

- Carry a spare wheel and all the tools you will need to change it.

Trailing checklist

Going overseas

One of the great advantages of a boat on a trailer is the freedom to go to different ports and overseas.

Rules and regulations change frequently, so contact the tourist and motoring authorities for the countries you intend trailing. While each country's regulations vary slightly, there are some common requirements that you must adhere, irrespective of the country you are travelling to.

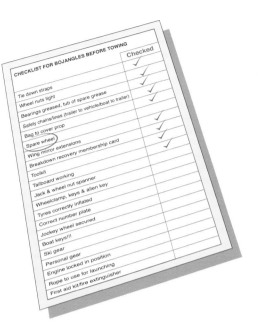

CHECKLIST FOR BOJANGLES BEFORE TOWING — Checked

- Tie down straps
- Wheel nuts tight
- Bearings greased, tub of spare grease
- Safety chains/lines (trailer to vehicle/boat to trailer)
- Bag to cover prop
- Spare wheel
- Wing mirror extensions
- Breakdown recovery membership card
- Toolkit
- Tailboard working
- Jack & wheel nut spanner
- Wheelclamp, keys & allen key
- Tyres correctly inflated
- Correct number plate
- Jockey wheel secured
- Boat keys!!!
- Ski gear
- Personal gear
- Engine locked in position
- Rope to use for launching
- First aid kit/fire extinguisher

The tow vehicle

- Original insurance documents and overseas car and trailer insurance documents.
- The original registration documents for the vehicle.
- A set of spare bulbs and a warning triangle.

The boat

- The original sale documents to show tax has been paid.
- Insurance documentation.
- Make sure the boat's insurance cover is extended both for trailing and its use and mooring at the intended destination.
- Flare transportation could cause problems, as some countries require a firearms certificate for certain types of flare.

The crew

- A VHF certificate is recommended and is mandatory in some countries.
- Visas, if relevant.
- Most countries require an International Certificate of Competence (ICC) and some require a higher qualification. On inland waterways in Europe the CEVNI qualification will be required.
- Contact the country's National Boating authority for details of compulsory certification required.

22 | Buying and Owning a Boat

For most people, buying a boat is a considerable investment. However, in contrast to buying a house or car, the process can be very simple but you need to be aware of some of the pitfalls, especially when confirming ownership.

- Do your research - use website forums to learn of other people's views and experiences. Build up background knowledge of the type of boat you want to buy.

- Make sure the boat is suitable for its intended use. Planning and forethought will prevent you investing in a boat that you quickly 'outgrow'.

- Check magazines for a boat test on the boat you are interested in, many sell back issues of boat tests.

- Always seek proof of ownership via original invoices. As with a car a good service history and receipts indicates a good ownership trail.

- If buying from a dealer, is it a brokerage boat or one of their own craft? If it is their own boat you will have protection under the Sale of Goods Act.

- Establish that no finance company has a charge or ownership right over the vessel.

- Invest in a hull and engine survey – damaged and worn engines can be extremely expensive to fix.

- A 'low mileage' boat is not always the best. A boat that has been well looked after and run regularly can be a very good buy.

Insurance

Once you have bought your boat, insure it. Most marinas and harbours stipulate that you must be insured to keep your boat there.

Storage

Smaller boats are often stored on trailers, therefore trailing from home becomes an option. Many boatyards offer 'store and slip' facilities. Increasingly popular is storing your craft on a rack system where a forklift retrieves your boat then launches it when required. Keeping a boat out of the water removes the need for antifouling and allows it to dry out when not in use.

Larger boats are usually kept afloat in marinas or on moorings, although even boats up to 10m can be kept on racking systems.

Storage costs vary enormously. Popular marinas and storage sites are far more expensive than boatyards in less congested boating areas. Drying berths, buoys and pile moorings are all slightly cheaper than a marina but at the cost of convenience.

Boat care

Boat care is largely a matter of common sense:

- Wash the boat after each outing to remove salt deposits.
- If possible, flush water through the engine water intakes to avoid salt crystallisation in the cooling pipes.
- Keep batteries charged through the winter (remove them if they are not being used).
- Grease battery terminals with petroleum jelly to ensure the electrical connections remain good.
- Spray the electrics with a water repellent spray to keep water out.
- Consider spraying other exposed parts with a silicone spray.

Service intervals for engines vary according to the manufacturers' recommendations. High-usage boats may need to be serviced more than once a year, whereas boats used less frequently benefit from an end of season service and winterisation if they are not to be used during the winter.

23 | SOLAS V

Worldwide all vessels need to comply with these regulations.

The exact wording of the regulations is used with some explanatory notes provided by the RYA.

• **Radar Reflector -** Regulation 19.2.1.7.

All ships shall have, if less than 150 gross registered tonnes and if practicable, a radar reflector or other means, to enable detection by ships navigating by radar at both 9 and 3 GHz.

RYA note: 'When practicable' means that if you can carry a radar reflector, you should. Both passive radar reflectors and active devices are available.

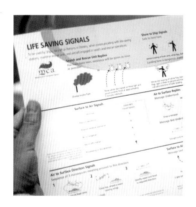

• **Life-saving Signals -** Regulation 29.

An illustrated table describing the life-saving signals shall be readily available to the officer of the watch on every ship to which this chapter applies. The signals shall be used by ships or persons in distress when communicating with life-saving stations, maritime rescue units and aircraft engaged in SAR ops.

RYA note: Keeping this table on board will mean that you comply with this regulation - the table can be found on pages 120/121.

• **Danger messages -** Regulation 31.

Masters are to communicate information on navigational dangers. These include, for example, a dangerous derelict or other dangerous obstructions, tropical storms, winds of Force 10 or more for which no warning has been received. The form that information is sent is not obligatory and it can be transmitted in plain language or using the International Code of Signals. Contracting governments must promulgate any danger information received and messages must be free of charge to ships.

RYA note: This regulation basically means that you, as skipper, have a responsibility to pass on information about navigation dangers to the Coastguard by any means that you can.

- **Danger messages** - Regulation 32.

This regulation deals with the kind of information required in danger messages. It also has examples of typical danger messages.

RYA note: This regulation means that you should pass on sufficient information about any navigation dangers you experience or witness (For example: position, nature of danger, time seen/witnessed, any other useful information) to enable other shipping in the area to avoid it.

- **Distress messages** - obligations and procedures - Regulation 33.

Masters are obliged to respond to distress messages from any source. Ships can be requisitioned by the master of a ship in distress or the Search and Rescue (SAR) authorities.

RYA note: This regulation reinforces the duty of skippers to respond to any distress messages they hear.

Safe navigation and avoidance of dangerous situations - Regulation 34.

Voyage planning is required on all vessels that go to sea. "Going to sea is defined as proceeding outside of categorized waters". You can get more information about what constitutes categorised waters from the MCA and the RYA.
MCA guidance notes say for 'small craft and pleasure vessels, the degree of voyage planning will be dependent on the size of vessel, its crew and the length of the voyage'. The MCA says that it 'expects all mariners to make a careful assessment of any proposed voyage taking into account all dangers to navigation, weather forecasts, tidal predictions and other relevant factors including the competence of the crew'.

RYA note: Skippers should note that this regulation changes the status of passage planning on small boats from simply good practice to a requirement under UK law. No formal written plan is required and there is no set format. Anyone who goes on an RYA practical course will be confident of their ability to plan a cruise competently. Anyone who is not confident of their passage planning ability should take a suitable RYA practical course. (see inside back cover for more details).

Misuse of ditress signals - Regulation 35.

"Distress signals only to be used for the proper purpose".

RYA note: This regulation reinforces the fact that distress signals have a life saving role and should not be misused.

24 | Life Saving Signals

To be used by Ships, Aircraft or Persons in Distress.

Maritime and Coastguard Agency

Search and Rescue Unit Replies
You have been seen, assistance will be given as soon as possible.

OR

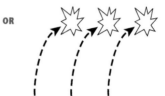

Orange smoke flare.

Three white star signals or three light and sound rockets fired at approximately 1 minute intervals.

Surface to Air Signals

Note: Use International Code of Signal by means of lights or flags or by laying out the symbol on the deck or ground with items which have a high contrast to the background.

Message	International Code of Signals		ICAO Visual Signals
I require assistance	V	✕ ···▬	V
I require medical assistance	W	▣ ▬·▬▬	X
No or negative	N	▨ ▬·	N
Yes or affirmative	C	▤ ▬·▬·	Y
Proceeding in this direction			↑

Air to Surface Direction Signals
Sequence of 3 manoeuvres meaning proceed to this direction.

1

Circle vessel at least once.

2

Cross low, ahead a vessel rocking wings.

3

Overfly vessel and head in required direction.

Your assistance is no longer required.

Cross low, astern of vessel rocking wings.

Note: As a non preferred alternative to rocking wings, varying engine tone or volume may be used.

Shore to Ship Signals

Safe to land here.

OR

K

Vertical waving of both arms, white flag, light or flare.

Morse code signal by light or sound.

Landing here is dangerous. Additional signals mean safer landing in direction indicated.

OR

S: •••
Morse code signals by light or sound.

R: •—•
Land to the right of your current heading.

L: •—••
Land to the left of your current heading.

Horizontal waving of white flag, light or flare.
Putting one flag, light or flare on ground and moving
off with a second indicates direction of safer landing.

Air to Surface Replies

Message Understood.

 OR **OR**  **OR**

T **OR** •—•
R

Drop a message.   Rocking wings.   Flashing landing or navigation lights on and off twice.   Morse code signal by light.

Message Not Understood – Repeat.

 OR  **OR**
•—•   •—•   —
R   P   T

Straight and level flight.   Circling.   Morse code signal by light.

Surface to Air Replies

Message Understood – I will comply.

 **OR** **OR**
—
T

Change course
to required direction.   Morse code signal by light.   Code & answering pendant "Close Up".

I am unable to comply.

OR

—•
N

Note: Use the signal most appropriate
to prevailing conditions,

Morse code signal by light.   International flag "N".

Notes

The RYA Motor Cruising & Yachtmaster Scheme

Helping you get started and get going - whatever your age or experience.

Helmsman

A two day introduction to motor cruising on a motor vessel. Learn basic boat handling, rule of the road, man over board and be made aware of safety considerations on board.

Day Skipper Shorebased

A comprehensive introduction to chartwork, navigation, meteorology and basic seamanship.

Day Skipper Practical

Pilotage, navigation, seamanship and boat handling up to the standard required to skipper a motor vessel safely, by day in familiar waters.

Coastal Skipper / Yachtmaster Offshore Shorebased

Offshore & coastal navigation, pilotage and meteorology.

Coastal Skipper Practical

Skills and techniques required to skipper a motor cruiser safely on coastal and offshore passages b day and night.

One Day Shorebased Courses

One day theory courses on
VHF Radio
First Aid
Diesel Engine Maintenance
Sea Survival and Radar

RYA/MCA Coastal Skipper*
RYA/MCA Yachtmaster Offshore*
RYA/MCA Yachtmaster Ocean*
*Certificates of Competence

These are gained by examination and are conducted by RYA Yachtmaster Examiners. Examinations are open to anyone with the required experience.

RYA courses are safe, informative and enjoyable. They are run at inspected Training Centres by qualified instructors; look for the tick mark logo.

RYA

For more information visit
www.rya.org.uk